"Todd Hunter's journey—unlike that of the 1980s 'evangelicals on the Canterbury Trail'—is a missional merging of Anglican resources and church-planting passion. Free of romanticized illusions, he offers a clear-eyed appreciation of the Anglican potential for mission after modernity."

**David Neff,** editor in chief and vice president, Christianity Today Media Group

"Todd's story is a fascinating, moving, honest and often very funny account of what God can do with one of his servants committed to growing his kingdom today. . . . Very inspiring."

**J. A. K. Millar,** vicar, Tollington Park, and assistant bishop, London

"You hold in your hand a thoughtful and candid explanation of the many events and people that God used to draw a veteran evangelical church planter like Todd Hunter into the world and the witness of the Anglican church. One part autobiography and one part apologia, this book provides an 'outsider's' perspective on the richness of authentic Anglicanism, and the treasures of this particular branch of the Christian church that have captured his heart and made him, in his own words, an 'accidental Anglican.' In telling this story, Todd challenges us all to begin to connect the dots in our own lives and discover the powerful, if seemingly accidental, calling that God has for each of us."

**Chuck Murphy,** chairman, The Anglican Mission

"Todd is a missionary and knows the attraction of 'ancient future' in today's culture. This remarkable book tells a remarkable story. A story of how Todd became an Anglican bishop. I was gripped as he uncovers the treasures of this ancient spiritual pipeline. So gripped, it reminded me why I'm an Anglican! This is a deeply personal story, written by an amazing man. It will challenge and inspire."

**Mark Russell,** CEO, Church Army, and member of the Archbishops' Council of the Church of England

"Todd Hunter's passion for church growth—and his many insights into how it can be achieved—has had a profound influence on many church leaders around the world. His story is a fascinating one."

**Nicky Gumbel,** vicar of Holy Trinity Brompton Church and developer of The Alpha Course

# The
# Accidental
# Anglican

*The Surprising Appeal*
*of the Liturgical Church*

# Todd D. Hunter

Foreword by J. I. Packer

IVP Books
An imprint of InterVarsity Press
Downers Grove, Illinois

InterVarsity Press
P.O. Box 1400, Downers Grove, IL 60515-1426
World Wide Web: www.ivpress.com
E-mail: email@ivpress.com

InterVarsity Press® is the book-publishing division of InterVarsity Christian Fellowship/USA®, a movement of students and faculty active on campus at hundreds of universities, colleges and schools of nursing in the United States of America, and a member movement of the International Fellowship of Evangelical Students. For information about local and regional activities, write Public Relations Dept., InterVarsity Christian Fellowship/USA, 6400 Schroeder Rd., P.O. Box 7895, Madison, WI 53707-7895, or visit the IVCF website at <www.intervarsity.org>.

All Scripture quotations, unless otherwise indicated, are taken from the The Message. Copyright © 1993, 1994, 1995, 1996, 2000, 2001, 2002. Used by permission of NavPress Publishing Group. All rights reserved.

Design: Cindy Kiple
Images: AngusImages

ISBN 978-0-8308-3839-4

Printed in the United States of America ∞

 InterVarsity Press is committed to protecting the environment and to the responsible use of natural resources. As a member of Green Press Initiative we use recycled paper whenever possible. To learn more about the Green Press Initiative, visit <www.greenpressinitiative.org>.

**Library of Congress Cataloging-in-Publication Data**

Hunter, Todd D., 1956-
    The accidental Anglican: the surprising appeal of the liturgical church / Todd D. Hunter.
        p. cm.
    Includes bibliographical references (p.      ).
    ISBN 978-0-8308-3839-4 (pbk.: alk paper)
    1. Hunter, Todd D., 1956- 2. Anglican Mission in the Americas. 3. Missionaries—United States—Biography. 4. Anglican converts—United States—Biography. 5. Province of the Anglican Church of Rwanda—Bishops—Biography. I. Title.
    BV2765.5.H86A3 2010
    266'.3092—dc22
    [B]

                                                                    2010024965

| P | 17 | 16 | 15 | 14 | 13 | 12 | 11 | 10 | 9 | 8 | 7 | 6 | 5 | 4 | 3 | 2 | 1 |
| Y | 24 | 23 | 22 | 21 | 20 | 19 | 18 | 17 | 16 | 15 | 14 | 13 | 12 | 11 | 10 |

*For Archbishop Emmanuel Kolini*

*and Bishop John Rucyahana*

*These men embody Christlike leadership.*

*They live and lead for the sake of others.*

# Contents

Foreword by J. I. Packer . . . . . . . . . . . . . . . . . 9

Preface . . . . . . . . . . . . . . . . . . . . . . . . . 13

**Part One: How I Became the Accidental Bishop**

  1 Life on My Own Terms . . . . . . . . . . . . . 19

  2 Liturgical Leanings . . . . . . . . . . . . . . . . 27

  3 Accidental Connections . . . . . . . . . . . . . 34

  4 Shaping a Faith: *J. I. Packer* . . . . . . . . . . . 40

  5 What Is a Rector? *The Influence of John Stott*. . . 46

  6 Following the Holy Spirit in Anglicanism . . . . 55

  7 Ordained a Deacon and Priest . . . . . . . . . 59

  8 Giving and Receiving the Eucharist. . . . . . . 66

  9 Consecrated as a Bishop. . . . . . . . . . . . . 71

**Part Two: What I Like About Anglicanism**

10 A Story to Embody: *N. T. Wright* . . . . . . . . 83

11 Anglicanism and the Kingdom of God . . . . . . 90

12 The Anglican Evangelistic Tradition . . . . . . 94

13 Anglican Leadership: *Emmanuel Kolini
   and John Rucyahana* . . . . . . . . . . . . . . . 104

14 The Spirit of Anglicanism: *A Sweet Reasonableness* 108

15 The Anglican Treasure Chest . . . . . . . . . . 113

Conclusion: *From Accidental to Purposeful* . . . . . . 120

Acknowledgments . . . . . . . . . . . . . . . . . . . 127

A Word from the Author . . . . . . . . . . . . . . . 131

Notes . . . . . . . . . . . . . . . . . . . . . . . . . 133

# Foreword

For a moment, let us all *play*. (Eh? Yeah.)

Imagine the following: Before you lies a new edition of Kenneth Grahame's classic for children from nine to ninety, *The Wind in the Willows*, in which Mole realizes the richness of the riverbank and Mr. Toad tastes the boomeranging trauma of unbridled locomotion. You open the book, and the first thing you see is a foreword, a set of remarks as from an authority introducing the book and celebrating it as a tale for our times, signed by Ratty. Having flipped through it, you move into the book itself and find to your surprise that Ratty is one of the characters in Grahame's story.

So what do you make of that?

A parallel problem faces you here and now, for you will meet me, who am responding to Bishop Todd Hunter's request for a foreword, as a character in his story. What to do? I can only act as if it isn't so and do my job as an introducer as I would do it anyway, never mind the things—kindly things, in fact—that he has written about me.

Todd Hunter is a veteran church planter from the Calvary Chapel-Vineyard world, a newish Anglican and a beginner bishop. The latter facts he milks to the utmost, and some of his stories are very funny. But the serious thrust of the book is to parade the resources he has found in Anglicanism for planting and nurturing churches on America's West Coast, which is his current task. In his estimate of what he finally calls the Anglican treasure chest I, a cradle Anglican who am now a converted and convictional one, resonate with him as enthusiastically as ever a man could, and it is from that standpoint that I want to commend his book.

I see the historic Christian church as like the Mississippi river. Along the edge are reed beds, mud flats, bayous leading nowhere and a good deal of stagnant water. Out in the main channel, however, the water flows steadily forward, and I see the Anglicanism of the past half-millennium decisively reformed and then periodically renewed in its authentic evangelical direction, as belonging to that main stream. I have, indeed, been privileged to live in one of the renewal eras; an era that, despite disruptions, continues to grow in strength and into which it is a joy now to welcome Todd.

What does ideal Anglicanism—treasure-chest Anglicanism, as Todd might call it—look like? The first thing to say is that it is Bible-based and Bible-oriented in the magisterial sense formulated fifty years ago by Bishop Stephen Neill: show us anything the Bible teaches that we are not teaching, and we will teach it; show us anything we are teaching that the Bible does not teach, and we will cut it out.

Then, Anglicanism is catholic, in the sense of being determined to preserve and practice the faith in its fullness, and to that end learn all that can be learned from the Christian past (the Creeds and the theologians), and also from what goes on in the Christian present within and outside the Anglican fellowship. With that, however, Anglicanism is Protestant, in the sense of being committed to use Scripture to correct past mistakes and reformulate distorted beliefs.

Furthermore, Anglicanism is resolutely Christ-centered, focusing always on his death and resurrection, his kingdom and his church, his gospel and the mission of the triune God, in which he himself and his claims are central. Also Anglicanism appreciates the devotional depth of its inherited liturgy, the didactic fruitfulness of its set lectionary and the need in nurture to promote in parallel both the inward journey of deepening fellowship with God and the outward journey of witnessing with wisdom, reaching out with love into our lost world, pointing the spiritually blind to Christ and setting forth a rational Christian humanism to counter the dehumanizing secular humanisms that the world constantly comes up with. Ideal Anglicanism is both pastoral and practical, linking together spiritual worship, work, wisdom and warfare, and looking first and foremost to its bishops for leadership in fulfilling this agenda.

Todd Hunter's book makes it plain that he discerns and embraces all of this ideal. So I may, I think, boldly say: hail to you, Bishop Mole! Ratty salutes you! Accidental Anglican you may be, but it is real, rich Anglicanism that you perceive and pursue. May your ministry among us be gloriously blessed.

*J. I. Packer*

# Preface

I am not famous. Just ask my teenaged daughter.

The only prominence I have is in my own mind, in my momentary lapses into self-importance. Thus I would never presume to write an autobiography as if I were astronaut Neil Armstrong or the Queen of England. Happily that is not the kind of book you now hold in your hands. I tell this story not because I think people are all that curious about me but because telling the truth, being genuine about myself, can have an explicative and orienting power for others. By *truth* I don't mean just the facts or that which is not false, spun or covered up. That is a given.

I shoot for something higher than mere facts in this book. My goal in telling this story is that you have some "Aha! I get it" moments for your own life as you explore the meaning and power of liturgical worship. I hope the truth of my story informs your own story, fills you with courage to follow your path and calls to mind those who have been guides for you, though maybe unnoticed until now.

## LITURGICALLY SEEKING

There is something in the air today, something in the spirit of our age, something in the Spirit that is leading thousands, maybe millions, of people to reconsider liturgical forms of worship. Liturgical seekers cherish the confidence that comes from historical connectedness, from theology that is not tied to the whims of contemporary culture but to apostolic-era understandings of Christian faith and practice. Our frantic lives make us yearn for rhythms and routines that build the spiritual health we seek. For many of us the architecture, theater seating and structure of our former churches said to us, "Sit back, relax and receive what comes to you from the stage." While having no need to criticize that, there is a hunger in many churchgoers today for a Sunday ethos that says, "Sit up, be alert and participate."

The liturgy, being the *work* or *participation* of the people, does just that. Furthermore, it fosters in us and connects us to a life of participation with the Holy Spirit in the 167 hours a week we are not in church. It teaches us weekly to love our neighbors, to be alert to the story of Scripture we read via the lectionary. The Eucharist feeds us on the resurrected Christ, imparting to us eternal life that spills over for the sake of others.

This is not a book that dissects the theology of the various groups I have had the privilege to serve. In fact, my trek to the Anglican Church was sheer calling. It had nothing to do with theological or ecclesiastical problems with the Jesus People or the Vineyard. My experience was more like falling in love with and marrying a long-standing friend I thought was "just a friend."

This book reveals the reality and benefit of unrecognized guides. Though rugged and zealous individualism is normative today, I think it is a crock. The life and work of other Anglican leaders largely shaped my decision to plant hundreds of Anglican churches and to be their missionary bishop.

No one lives completely unaffected by others. We all learn how to live from someone. Even individualists learn the values of individualism from someone else and are, consciously or not, modeling or mimicking that person's example. The key question to ponder is: Did we *choose* people to learn from, or have we *drifted* into learning from them?

## WAS IT AN ACCIDENT?

I chose. I chose to follow Jesus. I chose to follow him because I think he knows more about doing life in the image of God than anyone who has ever lived. I also chose to follow the example of the people I will introduce you to in this book.

It is in this sense that I am in no way an *accidental* bishop. I chose. I am not a victim of others. I have benefited from others and from God's leading in ways that I simply did not anticipate. In my case *accidental* means blessed, lucky and fortunate—kind of like a Little Leaguer who *accidentally* hits a pitch with his eyes closed. *Accidental* in this context is just a playful way of saying, "I didn't see it coming!"

In addition, I am neither a victim of nor the architect of this story. I am more like a young boy at a Six Flags amusement park, staring up at the huge twisting, looping, lose-your-corn-dog-and-root-beer roller coaster. Sizing up the intoxicating fusion of thrill and buzz with apprehension and fear, I decide to say, "Mom, hold my popcorn. I'm goin' on!"

Yep, I *decided* to go on this ride. I take responsibility for it—especially for any of its negative and unintended consequences. But as a devout follower of Jesus, I am more than happy to give

God credit for all the good. I am clearheaded about this: I did not design or build the ride. If it turns out to be a great ride, well, all glory to God.

## LOOKING BACKWARDS

There are some things we can only know by looking backwards. To do that I'm going to clean off all the windows of my past and let you peer into the crucial, life-shaping events of my life. I am going to open wide the front door of my journey to introduce you to the key influencers who, in hindsight, set me up to be an accidental Anglican. As we go along, I will point out bits of Anglican history and theology, and their influence on my work as a missionary bishop. I will recall the Anglican leaders who have shaped my thinking and practice. I'll describe for you how these leaders helped develop in my mind a vision for the role Anglican history, theology and practice can play in contemporary society.

The movie character Forrest Gump famously said, "Life [is] like a box of chocolates. You never know what you're gonna get." I can relate. But for me another metaphor works better: Life is like a box of shiny bits of glass—discern them long enough and a beautiful mosaic appears.

I have been blessed by great people who have influenced me and set me up for an unforeseen, but now greatly loved, role as a missionary bishop sent from the Anglican Church of Rwanda to the West Coast of America. Our goal is to start hundreds of Anglican churches whose chief values and practices revolve around the notion of being *churches for the sake of others*.

But to become an accidental Anglican bishop, I first had to confront some on-purpose, wrong-headed selfishness on my part.

PART ONE

# How I Became
# the Accidental Bishop

# I

# Life on My Own Terms

In 2008, at age fifty-two, I was trying to retire—in a manner of speaking. I was beat half-dead by the grind of sitting in air-planes and made sick by hotel rooms whose fruity air freshener was covering up the body odor from the guy who just checked out. (Typing this paragraph reminds me how much I was hop-ing to never see the inside of a commercial airplane or hotel room ever again!) I wanted life on my own terms.

While writing this book I have been splitting my time be-tween Eagle, Idaho, and Costa Mesa, California. But when this accidental journey began, before the church plant in Costa Mesa had been conceived in my mind, my heart was focused in the wonderful upstairs office in my home in Eagle, Idaho. Nearly two thousand books surround my desk and recliner. The pic-ture window above my desk yields a view of the beautiful Boise Mountains and the local ski resort—Bogus Basin. White win-ter, green spring, hazy summer and golden fall—the mountains treat me to shifting seasonal splendor.

With these glossy calendar-like pictures in my mind, I thought I had it all figured out. I would not actually retire in the sense of stop working, but I would arrange things so that *I* could set the conditions for my life. That was the crucial vision for me: *life on my own terms.* I was keenly focused on having no more hard decisions, no more boring meetings and no more travel—only what *I* wanted to do. I wanted to sit in my office, glance at the mountains, read, think, write, speak and teach—when and where I wanted.

I had come to the conclusion that I no longer had the will or the emotional and intellectual energy to deal with the inherent politics associated with any sort of religious leadership. I was tired of the rat race of planes, trains and automobiles—especially because those races always ended in yet another lonely, smelly hotel room.

I love the television commercial sponsored by GoToMeeting. Perhaps you've seen the guy throw lighter fluid on his travel bags and set them on fire with his BIC lighter, or the woman push her rental car into the riverbed. I feel a vivid and personal connection.

I've been in charge of something since I was a teenager—for thirty-four years. Now, I was tired of running organizations, tired of the politics, tired of the complex decisions and the fund-raising. Lest you think this chapter is one long whine, let me keep things real by giving you a peek into my heart and soul.

### JONAH-LIKE TEMPTATION

I confess, I have my moments when I want a ministry that costs me as little as my sense of right and wrong will allow. It is a genuine temptation—one of the strongest of my life.

I come from a generation in which *duty* is a dirty word. Obligation is for the old-fashioned or for the grace-challenged. Duty is way too puritanical. It feels like it sets *me* aside. And aren't *I* the most real and valuable part of all creation? "Come into the twenty-first century," many of us cry, "and get a good book on the freedom of grace." We say this as if grace has to do only with making us feel good about and ratifying our self-serving choices.

Well, I've got a good book on grace—Galatians. It is written by the original grace guy himself—the apostle Paul. His take on freedom and grace challenges me and speaks to many in my generation:

> It is absolutely clear that God has called you to a free life. Just make sure that you don't use this freedom as an excuse to do whatever you want to do and destroy your freedom. Rather, use your freedom to serve one another in love; that's how freedom grows. (Galatians 5:13)

Pleasure and recreation are deep things that call to the deep inner parts of most of us. *Responsibility* on the other hand is not intuitive or normative. It calls for some of the most mysterious and multilayered personal growth we will ever pursue. If you doubt it, interview someone who cares for others, such as police officers, nurses, schoolteachers or workplace supervisors. They will tell you that they daily have to set themselves aside and keep growing as persons to keep giving out to others.

My mind sometimes accuses me: *How can you be tempted to flee responsibility when you consider yourself a serious follower of Jesus?* James Lloyd Breck, a well-known Anglican leader in the 1800s, might say to reluctant church leaders like me: "It is base cowardice to run away from the church because she is not what she ought to be, and thereby leave her to those who care naught for her claims."

He is surely right. But this is also a man who once wrote to his bishop: "I have had enough of governing. A young man should never be permitted to exercise rule." And later to a friend: "I care not for being . . . the head. I have had enough of that for a lifetime." Perhaps many leaders have perplexing and clashing ideas going on in them. We leaders can be like computers trying to simultaneously run Windows, Mac OS and Linux, good but incompatible computer operating systems. Not a bright move. I can almost feel the lost information, the chin-in-the-hands and the tears-falling-on-the-keyboard crash coming on.

My temptation toward life on my own terms was powerful in the latter part of 2008. I had to admit it. But, from what I often hear from others, I've also got a lifelong track record of being a kind, loving and others-oriented person. I actually don't have a profound answer for why this is the case. I only have this explanation: I am not yet fully formed as a follower of Jesus.

Incredibly, in my malformed, misshapen inner self I sometimes even fall prey to atheism! I do—at least by one definition of atheism I have heard: Atheism is the thought that nothing good is going to happen here unless *I* make it happen. This kind of thinking is, like matches to lighter fluid, a sure-fire path to the kind of burnout that leads us to flee positions of responsibility.

My capacity for vision, my ability to see godly possibilities and my faith that such inspirations can come to pass, sometimes outrun my character. I feel no need to and cannot defend myself in this regard. But when I heard the voice of God say, "Todd, are you willing to consider that your multifaceted rationale for semi-retirement might actually be a convoluted means of sin and disobedience," I listened. And in the end I obeyed.

The weariness of being "the responsible one" rears up on bad days. But it's too bad for that broken part of me. I'm all in now. It's too late to turn back. I've entered the race for the last run of my life, and I intend to finish—and finish well.

## AN OFFICE OF SERVICE

Surprisingly, I am finishing as an Anglican bishop.

The ordained ministries of deacon, priest and bishop are emphasized in the Anglican Church, but not as a way to distinguish ourselves from other Christians. It's a way of describing Christlike service to others—both those in and outside of the church. Anglican priest and theologian Richard Hooker, a bright light in early Anglican history, is said to have believed that

> the [ordained] ministry serves the people of God. The fundamental order is that of deacon. Every priest, every bishop is first of all and always a deacon. Viewed thusly, the ordained ministry is subservient to the people and at its best it has always acknowledged that fact with gratitude.

That's the bit I realize I was missing—"always a deacon . . . always serving others." I was more like Moses, saying: "Lord, must I get water for these grumbling people again?" That was truly an *inconvenient truth* for me. I was looking for someone to give *me* water.

Me—a missionary bishop in the Anglican Church? Back in the game of church planting? Returning to one of the most responsible and risk-taking positions in the church world?

NOT OUT OF THE BLUE

What struck me as accidental—like the surprised *ouch!* we feel when we hit our head on a low doorway—was not an inadvertent occurrence to God at all. It was a burning bush moment. God looked past my weaknesses to reemploy my modest strengths. With his grace-filled, confidence-giving countenance on me, I could feel my zeal for ministry return. Like weed killer, God's presence and voice browned unwanted and dreaded weeds that choke out the desirable, growing and healthy parts of us. I could feel selfishness being killed—at least until the next cycle—and fertilizer being poured on the more desirable plants, such as faith, hope and love.

This was my journey back to faith and self-denial. The confidence and loyalty of faith, and the sacrifice and surrender of self-denial, are the foundations of obedience. They snuck up on me as if by accident, but in reality they were God-breathed.

Conversations, events and memories over the past ten months have shown me that my calling into the Anglican Mission in the Americas (theAM)—a missionary/church-planting movement sent from the Anglican Church of Rwanda and connected with the Anglican Church in North America (ACNA)—has not really come out of the blue. Reflecting back, I can now see a clear trajectory of events and people that prepared me to be an *accidental* bishop.

A BRIEF BACKGROUND

For those who do not know the outline and shape of my journey, the following is a bit of background and context.

*1976-1979.* I was converted in the Jesus Movement at the age of nineteen. I was, as was somewhat common those days, encouraged to begin ministering immediately. I taught my first Bible study in a home within weeks of my conversion. I taught the high school class at a Methodist church and became its youth pastor around the age of twenty.

*1979-1986.* By twenty-two I knew I wanted to start a church, and at twenty-three I moved with my wife, Debbie, and our closest friends, Tim and Susie, to start a Calvary Chapel church in Wheeling, West Virginia, which later became a Vineyard church. Though it is now thirty years since we moved from Wheeling to Southern California, we have never replaced the wonderful friends we made there.

*1987-1990.* At age thirty-one, in 1987, I was called by John Wimber to the Vineyard in Anaheim to help pastor that large and growing church, and to help with the start-up of the Association of Vineyard Churches USA.

*1991-1994.* After experiencing a few personal faith setbacks in the late eighties and early nineties, we moved in 1991 to Virginia Beach, Virginia, to take over a Vineyard church and to supervise Vineyard churches in the southern part of the East Coast.

We also helped to start seven other churches in those three years. In addition, after fifteen years in ministry, I finally attended seminary, receiving a master's degree in biblical studies from Regent University.

*1994-2001.* From 1994 to 1997 I was the National Coordinator of Vineyard Churches USA, and after the early death of John Wimber in November of 1997, I became the president of Vineyard Churches USA. I was only thirty-eight when I took the first role in the denominational headquarters. In 20/20 hindsight, I was too young to take such a role (too young to last in the job in any case).

It wasn't that I failed in the post. The board gave me consistently high marks in my annual reviews. But I got bored in the task. I missed church planting, evangelism and hands-on spiritual formation and preaching. In addition all the challenges and opportunities associated with postmodernism and post-Christendom were presenting themselves by the late nineties. I was engaged with these issues through my work with young church planters in the Vineyard.

In my mid-forties I had a choice to make: stay on the sidelines or get back into the game and help others in evangelism, church planting and spiritual formation in the early twenty-first century. I felt called to and chose the latter.

*2001-2004.* From the Vineyard I made my way to Allelon, which at the time was a coaching ministry for church planters founded by Mark Priddy. Allelon took my family from California to Idaho in 2003. At Allelon I engaged with church planters from all over the world who were trying to crack the code of being church in the cynical years of the early 2000s. During this time I pursued and completed a doctor of ministry degree at George Fox Evangelical Seminary in Portland, Oregon. I also began to teach as an adjunct professor at institutions like Fuller Seminary, Wheaton College and George Fox Evangelical Seminary.

*2004-2008.* I spent 2004-2008 as the executive director of Alpha USA, an evangelism course run in thousands of American churches. I have a huge amount of respect for The Alpha Course. However, by 2008 I found myself again wanting to do something different. I left Alpha not because of any disagreement but because I didn't feel that, being mismatched in terms of my gift mix, I was able to fully serve its needs.

This is where the story of the accidental Anglican begins.

# 2

# Liturgical Leanings

I am the type of guy who works so hard at being present to any given person or moment that I rarely take the time to write things down or take pictures. I do tend to later reflect deeply on things, but I am not a good journal or diary keeper. Thus as I started reminiscing and making notes for this book, I felt like a kid connecting the dots on the place mat at a family restaurant. You probably recall the delight: "Look at that—dots that make an elephant!"

As I've looked back over my life, something like that has happened to me: "Look at that—events and people that make an Anglican bishop!"

### THE INITIAL ATTRACTION

For example, a memory surfaced that reveals I had some liturgical leanings for quite some time before I joined the Anglican Mission. About eight years prior to joining the Anglican Mission, I started what I call "an attempt at alternative church, born from the angst of the early emerging church scene."

This godly little experiment of a church was populated mostly by ex-church people who thought of themselves as "church alumni." They were *been there, done that, graduated and looking for the next thing* people. In terms of body life, we had wonderful times exploring Quaker-like meetings in which everyone participated in spontaneous ways—which just proves that we were doing nothing really new. I am not sure we were even looking for new in the sense of "never tried," just different, something that would again give us hope in church. To this day the members of that little church are some of my best and most cherished friends.

While this church, which was trying to be nonchurch, was different in many ways, we were attracted to what some people were calling an "ancient-future" vibe. Thus, we asked a local Episcopal church if we could meet in their facility on Sunday evenings. It was an ideal, iconic building in my mind. Beautiful wood and stone everywhere. Religious symbols and icons tastefully decorated the room. The church was rarely used on Sunday nights. It was a win-win situation. We got the use of good facilities, and they got a little rent money.

Blessed Sacrament Church was remarkably generous and hospitable to a bunch of rough-around-the-edges, barely churched Christians. Like motorcycle gangs checking each other out, evidently we still had on enough spiritual leather and attitude to let our brothers and sisters at Blessed Sacrament know that while we were beat up, we were still "in."

Their rector even agreed to serve as my spiritual director for a period of time. He gave me my first copy of the Book of Common Prayer. It is still on my desk at home. While I've got some nerve-racking memories associated with Blessed Sacrament, I liked Father David very much and enjoyed our hours together. At Blessed Sacrament I had my first thought that someday I would be saying daily prayers with a group of Christians who were serious about the twin tracks of following Jesus: (1) spiritual formation into Christlikeness (2) for the sake of others.

Some Sunday evenings at Blessed Sacrament we met in the fellowship hall, other nights on the patio picnic tables around a meal. My personal favorites were the nights we met in the sanctuary. I loved the aroma created by decades of incense-filled worship. The icons and beautiful church furnishings seemed to draw me into a space that invited a sharp and reverent focus on God.

Somehow the evenings in the dimly lit sanctuary drew me out of an individualistic, *what do I get out of it* mentality to something that was communally connected to all the events, prayers, eucharistic celebrations and people that the burned incense had engulfed and surrounded. We often used various prayers from the Book of Common Prayer that resided in the pew racks. Most of us had never been in a church with pews and racks filled with prayer books, hymnals and Bibles. No worries. We were on an adventure, and the new surroundings were making inroads into what were up to then some fairly hard hearts.

My favorite moments were when we would all gather at the front of the altar rail, fifty or so of us in a tight group. Having read a closing prayer from the Book of Common Prayer, we would sing the Doxology—just raised and worshipful voices, no instruments. It gave me goose bumps then and is a wonderful memory now.

Warm moments like that marked our time at Blessed Sacrament. That is until we made a rookie mistake which shouted loudly that Christ Community Church had zero background in things liturgical. Our novice gaffe introduced us to a new phrase: *altar guild*. While I had a fuzzy memory from my Methodist upbringing, the thought still went through my head: *What the heck is an altar guild?*

An aside: Our new Anglican church plant in Costa Mesa is only five months old at this writing. And *I* am the altar guild chair. Does God pay people back for their sins? Theologically I think not. Obviously God is the Forgiver. But I must admit to laughing at the coincidence that now I am uptight about how our various altar elements are cared for! I now know how much work it takes, even in a small church, to take loving and reverent care of the altar. But at that point in my journey I was a greenhorn.

Thus I was anxious when my secretary told me that I had a phone message telling me that the chair of the altar guild had called to tell me that we had made a faux pas the prior Sunday night. I suddenly felt like I was being sent to the vice principal's office for my infraction of the rules.

*What could it be?* I wondered. Wanting to show our respect and gratitude for the use of the church facilities, we always cleaned up really well. We strived to leave the rooms and grounds as good or better than the way we found them. I quickly and nervously returned the call. The problem: sacred space and expensive candles. How was I to know? We could go anywhere in a Vineyard church. There were no holy barriers in converted warehouses.

The drama unfolded like this. We liked to turn the lights down and used lots of candlelight. Not being greedy or presumptuous, we brought in our own candles and stands. But one night while rummaging around the building during setup, we noticed a room called a sacristy—at least that is what I think it said. Sacristy, to our ears, was a slightly scary and medieval sounding term, but we were drawn to what we saw hanging on the wall just outside of it: two golden candle lighters. (Good thing this was a church and not a dungeon, or we would have been edgy.)

We didn't dare to open the forbidding and intimidating room with the sign on it, but the golden candle lighters outside the sacristy door, looking like giant fishhooks supported by wooden handles and with a bell welded to one side (a *snuffer* for those not familiar with these candle lighters) had drawn our attention to the various beautiful candles on the other side of the altar rail at the front of the church.

I am not 100 percent sure, but to this day I think we were okay as long as we stayed in the chancel area. Some traditions call this kind of area "ambulatory," so I guess it's okay to walk there. On the other hand, geographical terms describing the inside of a church were at that time still a little fuzzy to this Calvary Chapel/Vineyard boy. I was a bit like a pre-med student in his first anatomy class. I was getting it, but not yet enough to do surgery.

But I do now know this: though we did not transgress willfully, once we walked past the altar rail, not being in Holy Orders, we were truly and surely bad to the liturgical bone. It is not funny that we made this egregious trespass in a church called Blessed Sacrament. But in hindsight, it was instructive. I must have repented adequately, because God seems to have forgiven me enough to let me into his priestly order of servants. Now I can go anywhere I want in most church buildings. (Although, I did just recently cause another little stir at a Catholic retreat center, but I'll save that story for another book.)

Who knew candles could be so expensive? They're not too bad at Walmart. And I certainly didn't know how time consuming it is to keep up an altar and to change a couple dozen candles. Let's not even talk about the wax dripped on the holy fabric and wood—we had no idea that fabric could be holy and expensive and costly to wash and repair. I know now. I had a brief but passionate phone-based teacher, the servant of servants at Blessed Sacrament Church: the altar lady. I had messed with her world.

That one summer Sunday night was gorgeous and amazing. Every candle in the place was lit—including our brought-ins and the little votives in the stair-stepped racks deliberately and carefully placed around the room in front of icons. That service of Christ Community Church was like Advent, Christmas Eve, Epiphany, Easter and Pentecost all rolled into one big inferno emitting holy tongues of fire and blowing winds of incense. Surveying the aftermath, like a college student who opens the fridge to discover that her roommate ate her leftover Chinese food, the chair of the altar guild was aghast.

After this escapade our friends at Blessed Sacrament could be forgiven for thinking that I *must* indeed be an *accidental* bishop. I think we paid them for the candle use and fabric cleaning, but in the long run here is how I see it: they helped fund my early Anglican education, and I am forever and sincerely grateful for it.

## THE IMPORTANCE OF SYMBOLS

It is ironic that in trying so hard not to be a regular church I found myself attracted to the ancient symbols—the altar area, the candles, the incense and the prayer stations with icons and votives. I could feel the sacredness of the altar area. It alerted me to a desire for the sacred within me, something that moved beyond the contemporary familiarity with which we interacted with God. The candles reminded us that Jesus is the light of the world and we are

> here to be light, bringing out the God-colors in the world. God is not a secret to be kept. We're going public with this, as public as a city on a hill. If I make you light-bearers, you don't think I'm going to hide you under a bucket, do you? I'm putting you on a light stand. Now that I've put you there on a hilltop, on a light stand—shine! Keep open house; be generous with your lives. By opening up to others, you'll prompt people to open up with God, this generous Father in heaven. (Matthew 5:14-16)

I have to admit here that there are people who grew up around these liturgical trappings and found them unhelpfully familiar. Not being my experience, I cannot comment on it. I only know what is real for me: the world of liturgy and sacrament was restoring love and respect for God, and love and service to neighbor as God's light in the world—all so that others would come to faith in Jesus and follow him.

The gift of liturgy for the sake of others did not come to me impersonally, like a package left on the doorstep by FedEx. It was delivered to me over a long period of time in the loving hands of some amazing Anglican leaders. Let me now show you those important links and relationships.

# 3

# Accidental Connections

I didn't begin my relationship with the Anglican Mission with zero connection to Episcopalians and Anglicans. I had long friendships with Anglicans such as Bishops Sandy Millar and David Pytches from England, whom I genuinely liked and admired. I knew from a distance and reputation the Reverend David Watson and others. But I didn't enter discussions about being an Anglican in a completely positive frame of mind. Let me tell you why.

## MY ANGLICAN BEGINNINGS

In the late nineties I served on the board and executive committee of the National Association of Evangelicals. Additionally, I was often invited to various think tanks on the sociology and mission of the church. This honor was given me for one reason: I was the president of Vineyard Churches. Otherwise I would have never appeared on anyone's radar screen.

I knew my place in the cosmos. I was riding John Wimber's coattails. I always knew it. I sometimes chafed under it as a twenty- and thirtysomething young man trying to make his own place in the world. But it was never bad. It was a most potent, life-lifting relationship. John and I often talked about "my highest and best use before God," and at the end of the day I always knew he had my best interest at heart. Though I worked hard for him, cared what he thought about me and did as he pleased, I never felt *used*.

I remember one particular meeting especially well. Around the table were leaders of various denominations. Directly across from me were two or three Episcopalians. At every break they took up a long-running, rather heated argument about "the 1979 version of the Book of Common Prayer."

Some background on the Book of Common Prayer is in order here. The Anglican Church and its Episcopal counterpart in the Americas have always been largely defined by their forms and practices. For hundreds of years those observances have been codified in the Book of Common Prayer. From 1928 until the early 1970s everyone used the 1928 edition. When a push came to update the Book of Common Prayer, as is typical, conservative and liberal sides formed, and loud and long arguments ensued—which takes us back to the meeting I was attending.

You might be surprised for me to say that, sitting there in my Hawaiian shirt—the Vineyard uniform—I didn't even know what a prayer book was. I certainly would not have known there was a 1979 version which might spark so much anxious energy. Of course, I now know a little about the issues surrounding various versions. But I must confess it took me a few months and a few gentle corrections from Bishop Charles Murphy to stop calling it the "Common Book of Prayer."

All I knew at the time, observing and hearing my colleagues across the table, was that I was like the Pharisee in the Bible, thanking God I was not an Anglican who had to argue about prayer books! I swore then and there to never be one.

**MY WAY?**

As my conversations with the Anglican Mission began, I was still trying to have life on my terms, *my way*. I knew I wanted to teach, but turned down two offers to be a dean. I knew I could help certain ministries as a consultant, but I didn't want to lead as a CEO. I was still interested in the church and evangelism, but I didn't want to lead another parachurch ministry.

Most important, though, I knew one other thing that in hindsight preserved my calling from God. I did not want to be a loner. I could see no benefit in being outside the church. I wanted to express my gifts and serve others from within a community of faith—a local church. No matter what I might do with writing, speaking, consulting or teaching, I wanted to work from within a church. Thus I started toying with the idea of being a teaching pastor somewhere.

Through a mutual friend, word of my desire got to my colleague Tony Baron. The day I talked to Tony, then rector of St. Anne's Anglican Church in Oceanside, California, he told me he was praying with his congregation about starting a daughter church in Carlsbad, California. Tony, knowing that I had been involved in church planting for many years, said, "Why don't you come help us start this new church?"

This made some sense, but mostly for geographic reasons. Debbie and our daughter, Carol, longed to move back to Southern California. Our families and old friends were there, Carol wanted to go to college there, and my son, Jonathan, was in culinary school and working in a restaurant there as well.

However, a thought flashed through my mind: *Church planting, I know what that takes. It sounds like being in charge of something again. I don't know if I want to do that.* But because

Tony and I had hit it off and it was clear we could be friends, I agreed to keep our conversation in mind, and even to come for a visit. But church planting did not seem promising.

This initial conversation took place in March. In April Debbie, Carol and I took a trip to Carlsbad to meet Tony, a few of his key leaders and his business partner, Art Barter. We enjoyed them all, and could see ourselves working in partnership with them. Except for this significant detail: my vision to have life on my own terms. What about semi-retirement in my upstairs office? Church planting was anything but slowing down!

In June I took one of my last trips as the executive director of Alpha. We were having a conference at Wheaton College, with a meeting of key Alpha pastors afterward. At the pastors' event, during a coffee break, I crossed paths with a friend I had not seen in a few months, Ron McCrary, former rector of Christ Church Anglican in the Kansas City area.

As is common in that kind of chance meeting, Ron said, "Hey Todd, what have you been up to?" I responded, "You won't believe this Ron, but I have been in discussion with Tony Baron about working with him to start a church in Carlsbad, California." The "you won't believe this" tone in my voice and the amazed look in my eyes were designed to carry the bolt-out-of-the-blue notion that *Todd Hunter—that old Calvary Chapel and Vineyard guy—was possibly planting an Anglican church!*

I mean—think about it—how does someone go from the Jesus Movement and the Vineyard to Anglicanism? While I am sure it is not unprecedented, it certainly doesn't happen every day in my circles, and not to someone who has had the high profile I had as the former president of Vineyard Churches.

With the coffee break over and the pastors' meeting about to start back up, just as Ron and I were about to end our conversation, he said to me "Do you mind if I tell my friends in the Anglican Mission about what you and Tony Baron are discussing? They may want to support you."

While I knew very little about the issues between the Episcopal Church and the more conservative churches who were then relating to bishops in Africa, Asia and Latin America, I had never heard of the Anglican Mission. But, being a lifelong church planter, I know what *support* means. It's code for money, and every church planter is looking for money! Even though I had not decided to plant a church with the Anglican Mission—or anyone for that matter—to cover any possible future bases I said, "Sure; go ahead."

A week or so later Ron set up a phone appointment for me with Ellis Brust, former president of the Anglican Mission, and H. Miller, then the director of leadership development, now the executive director. As we talked, I shared the vision Tony and I had been discussing. At some point in the middle of conversation, I remember saying something like, "Well, knowing me, if I start one church, I'll end up starting a lot more churches out of that church, because that is my habit and pattern."

We had a good enough chat that at some point it was suggested I come to Pawleys Island, South Carolina, for further discussion with Bishop Chuck Murphy, chairman of the Anglican Mission, primatial vicar (primary representative) in America to Archbishop Emmanuel Kolini of Rwanda.

## MEETING THE BISHOP

In mid-August 2008 I arrived at the appointed time for my meeting with Bishop Murphy, and after a brief tour of the building, I, along with a group of Anglican Mission leaders, was taken to a room off of the fellowship hall at All Saints Church. We settled into the comfortable seating and engaged in some small talk for a few minutes while waiting for Bishop Murphy to arrive.

When Bishop Murphy walks into a room, he commands attention. His tall frame, natty attire, bright eyes and awareness of others is obvious to anyone not asleep. I was certainly fully alert, knowing that my life could be at a critical crossroads. I was aware that a significant leader had just walked into the intersection of my work life.

For the next few hours we talked about what could happen on the West Coast. We dreamed out loud about starting new churches that brought together the best of the liturgical, evangelical and Spirit-filled streams—and in contemporary and missional ways. My new friends gave me my first lessons in Episcopalian, Anglican Church and Anglican Mission history, politics and mission. It was truly a delightful and informative day. I left the next morning feeling loved, respected and invited, but I still had no sense of leading from God.

I remember saying (and hoping no one would take it the wrong way), "I don't need you guys to plant ancient-future, missional, spiritual formation, Spirit-empowered churches. Why should I get in this big, fussy denominational mess?" So, I had no leading from God upon leaving Pawleys Island. In fact, *no leading from God* was about to dominate my life that summer.

Eventually, discernment came through the influence of people I trusted and admired. As I called to mind the Anglican leaders who had influenced my life, I began to see that I could possibly fit and make a positive contribution to mission in the Anglican Church. In the next chapters I'll introduce you to a couple of those influential mentors.

# 4

# Shaping a Faith

*J. I. Packer*

A number of Anglican thinkers and leaders have influenced my life. Though I was not a part of their tribe, they shaped my thinking about what Christians believe and practice, what it means to be a teacher and leader in the church, and how to comport oneself while doing so.

I am not alone in acknowledging help from others. It is most rare for anyone to be able to say, "I did this by myself." Ninety-nine percent of people who accomplish things of significance do so with the help of their background, their context and the people around them. An old saying notes, "If you ever see a turtle on a fence post, you know it didn't get there by itself." It's certainly true for this turtle.

The whole point of this book is that my journey into the Anglican Church was like someone putting pieces of colored glass on a table and arranging them into a stained-glass window through which I could see my way into the Church. One key bit of glass in the mosaic is J. I. Packer.

## MEET J. I. PACKER

Named by *Time* magazine in 2005 as one of the twenty-five most influential evangelicals, J. I. Packer may be best known for his influential book *Knowing God* published in 1973, just a few years before I came to faith. He has been a much sought-after speaker and lecturer. A prolific writer, he appeals to Christians from all walks of life. American historian Mark Noll wrote, "Packer's ability to address immensely important subjects in crisp, succinct sentences is one of the reasons why, both as an author and speaker, he has played such an important role among American evangelicals for four decades."

That's the bio, but it doesn't adequately reflect the influence or end product of Packer's life. Speaking just for myself, for more than three decades, beginning with reading *Knowing God* in the 1970s, and up to key personal meetings in 2009, Packer, with his simple, holy and mature reflections on all-things theological, has kept me grounded. To this day *Knowing God* is a great conversation partner for anyone willing to engage with a classic Christian worldview.

Interestingly, as Packer was having this big effect on my life, I never thought of him as an Anglican. Granted, I was particularly ignorant of religious facts when I came to faith, so all I knew was that Packer was English and one of the most influential evangelicals in the Western world. But I would not have known where he lived—the United Kingdom, Canada or the United States—or what he did for a living—teach or serve as a pastor and so on. I was in Calvary Chapel at the time. Because my Calvary friends gave me the book, I thought that Packer must be one of us—at least loosely so. It's a tad embarrassing to admit.

## A LIFELONG PURSUIT OF KNOWING GOD

Among many reasons I could list, Packer inhabits the Mount Rushmore of my Anglican influences because he is engaged in a lifelong quest to know God—as am I—and to let that knowledge shape and use him (and me) to help others know God as well.

Like many of my generation, my faith walk has gone okay, with predictable ups and downs. But in the late twentieth century came postmodernism, which said we could not *know* anything for sure. Equally or more alarming is the new atheism, a post-Christian attack that says knowing God is not even a decent, humanly helpful or morally good endeavor.

Packer's body of work is more valuable today than ever. He helps us to know not just *about* God but to know God personally. There is a huge difference—and one that is not always acknowledged. Think about this for a moment: I know *about* lots of people on the nightly news and magazine covers. But I do not know *them*. Knowing implies drawing close to someone, having an intimate, though not exhaustive, understanding of him or her. I don't have this kind of relational knowledge of Derek Jeter, Hillary Clinton, Sandra Bullock or George Clooney. But personal knowledge of God is available to all who seek it through Jesus, the Word and the Spirit.

## A LIFELONG PURSUIT OF HELPING PEOPLE KNOW GOD

Most evangelicals—whether they are Pentecostals, Baptists, Methodists, Presbyterians or Bible churchgoers—have read *Knowing God* and said, "Yep, that says it well for me. This *is* what we believe." This is no small feat. We evangelicals have no pope, no one to speak for us all. But for decades now, Packer's book has been a valued statement of basic Christian views of God and how to know him.

The *how* to know God part is crucial to evangelicalism today. I am aware that my generation of evangelicals has made a big deal out of having a "personal relationship with Jesus" through being born again. But this language has gotten stale. Many outsiders no longer find it understandable or compelling. They actually run from it in many cases.

But looking back to my first reading of Packer's *Knowing God*, I now know that I was experiencing my first bit of Anglican thinking—and more importantly the spirit of thoughtful Anglicanism. I realize that my literary introduction to Packer was one piece of a stained-glass window that was going to eventually look like Todd Hunter: *the accidental bishop*. But there was one more happy addition to the stained-glass window that occurred just before my consecration as a bishop.

The chairman of the Anglican Mission, Bishop Murphy, arranged for me to have a two-day meeting with J. I. Packer at Regent College in Vancouver, B.C. The stated reason for the extended personal conversation was to give me some training and background in evangelical Anglicanism. There may have been a bit of vetting going on as well, and if so, that is fine too. All I knew is that I was enormously grateful to Bishop Murphy for setting up the meeting and appreciative to Dr. Packer for agreeing to see me. Once the meeting was confirmed, as the weeks until we met unfolded, I created a list of questions I wanted to ask, issues I wanted to raise and ideas to discuss.

This being my first personal encounter with Packer, I didn't
know what to expect.

Surprisingly, he let me set the agenda for the two days. As we
worked through my list, I discovered in him the most amazing
combination of attributes. He has an amazing, encyclopedic
mind. I'd ask a question or throw out a thought, and after a ten
or fifteen second pause, Packer would deliver a well-composed
answer. Packer has uncommon intellectual gifts.

But what about the overall quality of the man? By the way
people in the parking lot, bookstore lobby and eating area
treated him, it was clear Dr. Packer didn't engage in any evangelical rock star behavior. Quite to the contrary, he was kind,
polite and engaging with others. This instantly put me at ease.
Dr. Packer is also patient—he has answered questions like mine
a thousand times. But throughout our two-day conversation it
seemed that he was answering *me*, not merely the question. I felt
as if he was trying to put himself in my shoes to answer my
questions in a manner that would be most helpful to a person
from my background and with my experiences. He was not just
turning out rote responses.

### IN THE TRIBE

I found Packer to be gentle, peaceful, kind and generous. He is
an icon of a loving and clear-thinking evangelical Anglican.
Looking back over decades of knowing English evangelicals, I
saw in J. I. Packer someone I should try to emulate as an Anglican bishop. If I couldn't pull that off, I would at least be happy
to say that I was of his tribe.

A English contemporary of J. I. Packer is John R. W. Stott. As
a young evangelical I often heard their names mentioned together.

I now see why. Packer and Stott represent the best of what it means to be an evangelical of the Anglican sort. Packer does so as a teacher and scholar, Stott as a pastor and scholar. Because I was about to become an Anglican pastor, I picked John Stott as a model of how to express love with clarity among a congregation of people, and to lovingly proclaim the gospel to the world's power brokers and among the middle class.

# 5

# What Is a Rector?

### The Influence of John Stott

From long experience I knew the routine activities of a *pastor*. But I was not sure what an Anglican *rector* or *vicar* was or what they did. I wondered: *What are the similarities? What are the differences?* To make matters more confusing, English and American Episcopalians used the words slightly differently. For our purposes here, think of *rector* and *vicar* as synonymous with *pastor*.

I found these words curious because in my former tribes we were all on a first-name basis. We didn't use titles like Father or Reverend to refer to anyone. It was just Chuck or Pastor Chuck (Smith) or John (Wimber).

I knew what my colleagues and I did during the week. We studied the Bible in preparation for sermons and tried to do the right things to grow our churches. But I often wondered what the "Fathers" in collars did.

## MEET JOHN R. W. STOTT

John Stott is for me a lifelong model of what it means to be a rector/pastor (who, by the way, in the tradition of English evangelicals wore suits and ties, not collars). His qualities of being, his keen mind, authentic spirituality and dedication to his congregation have shaped my imagination for a number of years.

Born in 1921 in London, John Stott was ordained in 1945 and has served most of his years in various roles at All Souls Church in London, the church of his youth. Conscientious and systematic preaching of the Word of God marked Stott's ministry at All Souls. "Every authentic ministry begins . . . with the conviction that we have been called to handle God's Word as its guardians and heralds," he wrote in his commentary on Thessalonians. "Our task is to keep it, study it, expound it, apply it, and obey it."

Through his preaching and writing, John Stott brought evangelicals to the forefront of the Church of England in the 1960s and eventually became a preeminent leader among evangelicals in Britain, the United States and around the world. He was the principal framer of the landmark Lausanne Covenant in 1974. The Lausanne Movement brought together thousands of Christian leaders from 150 nations and virtually all branches of Christianity to covenant around the themes and questions of the 1970s. Stott's leadership of the movement is the most visible part of his deep and wide international influence. He is a model world Christian.

Stott earned this distinction through his passion for missions and for investing in international pastors. From his professional budgets, such as ASIF (International Fellowship at All Souls), or from his own not-so-deep pockets, Stott purchased books and teaching materials for untold numbers of ministers around the world. He helped pay for seminary education for not a few needy ministers-in-training. This generosity was born from a life passion to equip global Anglican clergy with resources they needed to be effective and fruitful.

Stott holds honorary doctorates from schools in Britain, America and Canada. He is the author of more than fifty books, including *Basic Christianity*, which has sold over two-and-a-half million copies and has been translated into scores of languages.

Throughout the world, John Stott is warmly remembered for speaking at six Urbana Mission Conventions and for his many publications with InterVarsity Press. In many quarters he is *the* model of biblically based expository preaching. This humble man of prayer led his church into evangelistic practices long before anyone ever heard of seeker- or outreach-oriented churches. His work on discipleship preceded the recent buzz about spiritual formation by decades. Before anyone knew about church growth seminars, Stott was training his congregation to lead and serve according to their gifts. In short, it is hard to find a more influential evangelical pastor of his generation. He taught me one of the most powerful ministry-shaping paradigms for what it means to be the church and thus to be a leader in the church: "the gospel creates the church and the church spreads the gospel, and . . . the gospel shapes the church as the church seeks to live a life that is worthy of the gospel."

Stott announced his retirement from public ministry in 2007 at age eighty-eight. Having remained celibate his whole life, making Christ and the church his foci, he now resides in a retirement community for Anglican clergy.

Through his life John Stott models what it means for a pastor to stand in the midst of shifting culture and preach the Word of God. There is something about the mixture of kindness, love, respect for others and scholarship exemplified in Stott that provides solid foundation for the many tasks of pastoral ministry.

### TRUTH AND LOVE

Truth mixed with love is difficult to practice. We live in a world that is increasingly intolerant. We are losing our ability to talk to one another, and we need the voice and guidance of leaders like John Stott.

Do the Scriptures and the testimonies of millions of Christ followers give us a true picture of reality, about how things really are? This is important because no one would become a follower of Jesus if they thought he and the New Testament inauthentic. No one, for instance, would take piano lessons from someone who does not know the difference between B-flat and F-sharp. And no one would let someone manage his or her investments that did not know a stock from a bond. Either Jesus is in fact the "exact representation" of God (Hebrews 1:3) and God's kingdom, or he is not. There is no wiggle room here. Each of us must decide, not just for reasons of intellectual honesty but because it is the only basis on which we can trust him as our guide into reality as it is known and communicated by God.

When I was young, knowledge was thought of as a good, important and even indispensable friend. We hunted the Bible for all kinds of truth. Admittedly, sometimes an overly naive reading of a text led us astray. But that doesn't mean we can't know anything for sure about the Bible.

Today, however, suspicion, cynicism and open-mindedness have almost completely supplanted claims to knowledge. Presently, to be intelligent is to doubt. To have faith in something or someone, or to claim to know something, is boorish, monocultural, unenlightened or even hateful.

Thankfully, God occasionally anoints a pastor/rector who articulates with integrity the Christian faith in an intelligent, winsome and respectful manner. John Stott is such a man. True faith, in the sense of *confidence*, cannot be sustained without believing that we are acting on knowledge. Stott has spent a lifetime giving us knowledge of and about God. He has given us solid stuff to *act* on. He has intelligently and graciously given us the raw materials on which to build lives of faith, lives of Christian spirituality in the way of Jesus.

Stott is not only a first-rate scholar, but he lives what he knows to be true. His faith is marked by concrete assurance and confidence born from experiential knowledge of God, which he has passed on to me and other pastors around the world. His legacy is not just his knowledge, and not just his ability to write it down, but all of that wrapped up in his manner of living.

Stott's gifts and graces have been rumbling around in my mind for going on thirty-five years. When I found myself wandering into his tribe, as I called him to mind, I realized how much I have respected his model of life and ministry. But this is not just a moralistic, general observation to me. Let me tell you why.

### CHARACTER: THE HEART OF EFFECTIVE LEADERSHIP

What I am about to declare true about John Stott I could say about most of the notable English rectors I have known over the past decades, but is it exceptionally true about Stott: leadership that calls to and affects the deepest parts of others is rooted in an essential, indispensable quality of character. This loving moral fiber is to godly leadership what scent is to a fragrant rose. We can't see the inner place from which the perfumed aroma comes, but we know its goodness and beauty the moment the sweet or tangy air hits our nose. It draws us in. In fact, in an effort to get the full-blown smell, we sometimes lose our sense of space, our depth perception, and the pedals tickle our noses.

Stott has had that kind of leadership. People care what he thinks. His mix of decency and kindness, his biblical and theological understanding made him a sought-after counselor to Christian leaders of all kinds—Billy Graham included. Stott was to his generation of ministers what the old E. F. Hutton commercial portrayed: when Stott talked about something important, everyone listened. I witnessed first-hand how a few words of constructive criticism from Stott could get the attention of my early mentor, John Wimber. Wimber, based on temperament and convictions, was not given to caring much what others thought about him—not in a rude or haughty way; he just never thought much about it. But when Stott had some constructive criticism, you could see its effect on Wimber.

This kind of influence does not come from smarts alone. There is *godliness* to such authority, in the strictest sense of that term: virtue in a God-derived, God-oriented manner. Think about it: would you trust God if God were only smart and powerful? Or do you trust God because God is also *good*? Among his contemporaries Stott had both things in spades: smarts and goodness. I wonder if we realize how much we miss lions of decency and integrity like Stott.

#### BASIC CHRISTIANITY: A GENEROUS ORTHODOXY

As a young man I read Stott's legendary book *Basic Christianity*.

This renowned book trained a whole generation to think well about the deity and work of Christ, and how to share him with others. As a preacher I consulted his *Cross of Christ*. As social concern came closer to the top on evangelical agenda I found his Involvement books to be a model of thoughtful, clear, yet humble, engagement with the social and moral issues of our time. I had also used his commentaries on Scripture and had read or heard some of his sermons.

Reflecting on Stott's life and writing for this book I've come to think this: he was generous in his orthodoxy. Stott's generous yet conservative orthodoxy is an important model for my generation of Anglican pastors. We live in a day when, if actual behavior is the measurement, it is normative to hate or dismiss the parts of the church with whom we disagree. Stott's moderating voice between branches of the church teaches us opposites: love and connectivity.

We are in an era in which macho demagoguery and hubris-filled fighting among the women and men of the church is increasingly normal. Stott's life stands in the middle of all that like an ancient sculpture in a village square, unmoved by any force of nature, as a peacemaker, as a kind but honest conversation partner, always looking for common ground. Like Tom Wright, Stott has enjoyed deep, genuine friendships with those with whom he disagrees. Though a teacher more than a preacher, Stott is willing to not tie every one and everything down such that there is nothing more to learn from the Bible or from colleagues. He looks for common ground first, not difference. He is more interested in others than in his positioning in the eyes of critics.

His love and connectivity have at their core, at their starting place, a clear self-differentiation. Stott has remained strong in his own positions while being open to learn from others. He has maintained a profound commitment to Scripture and in-the-pail, historic Christian thinking. Displaying these traits, and as a trusted English leader, Stott helped to found "The Church of England Evangelical Council," the generous-spirited and biblically orthodox conversation of his generation.

Let's take a breath here from my applause of Stott. Some readers may need more than a breath; they may need a question answered: so what?

For me the "so what?" is this: I am not just reflecting on Stott—I am reflecting on the soil that gave rise to this oak tree of orthodox goodness. As I was making my way into Anglicanism, I thought not just of John Stott. My deeper reflections were along this line: Stott's life is a reflection of the best of Anglicanism—what I call in a later chapter *a sweet reasonableness.*

Anglicans at their historic best are not pugnacious, contentious, belligerent or loud-mouthed. Stott, in keeping with these family traits, is embracing, a warm conversation companion and *soft*-mouthed. Clear and confident, he has no need to be self-defensive. He easily accepts difference. Trusted Anglican colleagues tell me that these godly traits come in part from what English evangelicals sometimes call "Prayer Book" Anglicanism.

Here is the story as I understand it from afar: The Book of Common Prayer, chock-full of Scripture and in the lectionary pointing to the whole of Scripture, was for Stott and his generation of ministers the standardizing norm. They practically had it memorized. It was the both the *coffee* and the *shop*—the content and mode of conversation. This intuitive agreement stands in stark contrast to the media-driven posturing and positioning that often happens in the United States.

I find the English version of things eminently more attractive. It was to this accidental bishop a rose scent that led me into a worldwide garden called Anglicanism.

## HONORED TO BE A PASTOR LIKE HIM

John Stott is an intelligent, godly, gifted pastor who by his strength of character and keen biblical knowledge could hold positive sway over the major events and issues of his day. From a distance I have felt his grace-filled love of others. I have pictured his keen and focused mind. I am awed by his commitment to Jesus as reflected in his celibacy. I admire how much others respect him and how he uses that platform for the good of others, never for his own aggrandizement. Though I am not close in gifts or ability, when I was considering becoming an Anglican rector, John Stott routinely came to mind.

All of this tugged on my soul. Here was a model to follow. I would be honored to serve even in a small way in the same church as Stott. It would be a privilege. This drew me to the community of faith that formed Stott: the Anglican Church. By following the models of J. I. Packer and John Stott I had hope that I could fit well in this new tribe.

But I still had questions. I needed to know whether God was leading me to the Anglican Church. I did not process all this alone. My discernment process included many conversations with senior Anglican leaders—and it helped. But being trained in a conversational relationship with the Holy Spirit, I wanted to hear God's voice—the unmistakable tone and calm I had heard in the past calling me to prior engagements with ministry.

# 6

# Following the Holy Spirit in Anglicanism

Readers who know something about Vineyard churches will not be surprised that it was important to me to follow the leadership of the Holy Spirit as I journeyed toward the Anglican Church. In fact a Vineyard friend had a role to play in hearing from the Spirit.

Rose Madrid-Swetman is copastor with her husband, Rich, of a Vineyard church in Shoreline, Washington. When she heard that I was contemplating working with the Anglican Church, she recounted to me a vision she had received a few years earlier.

As you were telling me about the possibility of Carlsbad [working with Tony Baron] I was reminded of a dream I had about you when you first resigned from the Vineyard. You were in a liturgical type church, you were wearing a collar, you had several people with you, a lot of young people and some older as well. I remember coming there

on a Sunday a.m. and thinking, wow this is great! Todd is
in his element. I remember the feeling I had being there,
that it was a happening place, it was different (in the sense
that it was in a church building that in my dream represented liturgical style, high church).

What should I have made of that? That is book of Acts stuff!
Fortunately my background in both Calvary Chapel and the
Vineyard taught me to trust in and rely on the Holy Spirit working through the body of Christ. I took Rose's vision as a gift
from the Holy Spirit. I understood it to be a word of knowledge,
a word of wisdom, an insight of prophecy or discernment.
Whatever the precise definition, being early in the discernment
process, it was one of the big attention-getting moments in my
journey. Before hearing from Rose, I certainly never saw myself
as being "in my element" in that kind of setting. But now with a
couple years reflection I find I am living that vision from the
Holy Spirit.

## A MILLION-DOLLAR QUESTION

Of the many quizzical and challenging comments I received as
word got out that I was considering working with the Anglican
Mission, one stands out. I highlight this comment because the
probing question is so powerful and because of the respect I
have for the challenger and the Holy Spirit moment it brought.

One day while sitting in my office I was desperate to process
my possible journey into the Anglican world with someone.
I'd already bugged all my Alpha USA friends who were Anglican pastors, so I thought I should not wear out my welcome
with them. It was one of those moments when I wished John

Wimber was still alive. I could always count on him for king-dom-of-God advice.

Thinking about Wimber led me to think about a leader Wim-ber and I loved, respected and admired, Bishop Sandy Millar. After a twenty-year run, Sandy is now the former vicar of Holy Trinity Brompton in London. He is now in charge of an Angli-can Church plant at St. Mark's in Tollington Park. Simultane-ously he is a special bishop in the diocese of London, with the specific charge to plant churches that reach those outside the church and make them into disciples of Jesus in the power of the Holy Spirit.

Because I have known Sandy and his wife, Annette, off and on for more than twenty years, and because our paths crossed with some frequency while I worked with Alpha, I felt I could email him to see if we could make a phone appointment. I was pleased to get a quick reply, and we were on the phone within a few days.

Before I tell you Sandy's question, I should give you a bit of background. Sandy is, of course, not perfect. But it is rare to hear him say anything unkind or negative about anyone. He is bullish on the notion that if you can't say anything good, then don't say anything at all. Fine. Except that when we know some-thing negative needs to be said, he won't say it!

Second, Sandy is smart. He has a sharp mind, quick, effective and impressive. Furthermore, with Sandy, this comes wrapped in a socially elegant and genuinely spiritual package.

As typical of Sandy, when I told him I wanted his help, he as-sured me that he could be of no actual help, but that he was happy to talk. But while I was delighted to be talking to him, and while I knew he had practiced law for about a decade as a barrister, I was not ready for him to play the lawyer and ask all these probing questions: Why would anyone want to be an Anglican right now (that is, with all the upset then present in the Anglican world)? Why would you place yourself and your creative vision under a bishop who may tell you that you cannot do it? "Todd," he went on, "You're a Vineyard guy, and you are used to following the guidance of the Holy Spirit. Are you sure you have the patience for Episcopal polity?"

I had no answer. At least not nearly good enough to satisfy a bright guy like Sandy. So I think I just admitted as much to him and said, "I don't know Sandy, but I think the Holy Spirit may be calling me to do this."

"Well then," he responded with genuine kingdom-first (like his soul mate Wimber) joy, "End of the story. You must do what God is calling you to do even if it does not make perfect sense right now."

Great! Here we go.

# 7

# Ordained a Deacon and Priest

I'd like to say that I have been superhero courageous through my journey from the Jesus People to the Anglican Church. But the reality is that I've been a complex mix of motivations and emotions. Being a recovering perfectionist—and perfectionism is a potent Spirit-life killer—I have feared I might be doing wrong. But there has been an odd corresponding reality (and those who have ever taken a real risk will immediately feel my confusing pain). Accompanying the fear was the belief that I was doing the right thing.

Courage is not about never feeling the emotion of fear. It's finding the faith to do the best you see to do while fully experiencing the fear of being wide off the mark or getting it wrong. This fear walked hand-in-hand with me along my path to becoming an Anglican deacon, priest and bishop. The Anglican pastors who had befriended me during my time at Alpha must have grown tired of my incessant questioning: Is this right? Am I and the Anglican Church a good fit? Will this move be too controversial? Will I be able to make a positive kingdom-of-God impact?

### GETTING AN IMAGINATION FOR HOLY ORDERS

Most of us have seen the sign in a diner or in a forwarded email
that contains the well-known words attributed to Satchel Paige:

> Love like you've never been hurt.
> Work like you don't need the money.
> Dance like no one is watching.

Every time I see the saying, I experience it as a voice. I hear it
calling to a broken place in me. Such sentiment or opinion is on
the surface obviously right. But how do people like me, a complex mush of fear and adventuresome spirit, ever get there? I
have learned that this is the way forward: self-understanding
rooted in the knowledge that (1) I am created in the image of
God, (2) I am remade by the death and resurrection of Jesus,
and (3) I must grow through the grace-filled, grace-enabled historic Christian spiritual disciplines.

The day I met Bishop Chuck Murphy at Pawleys Island, I had
a revelation of sorts: I did not *need* to be in the Anglican Mission
to plant churches with liturgical, evangelical, spiritual formation and missional elements. I could have started a church like
that. I could have even attempted to start many churches using
that model. I did not need a new ordination as a deacon, priest
or bishop.

This did not involve any kind of arrogance or negative inde-
pendence. On the contrary, having that thought made clear to
me that my calling to the Anglican Mission was not a pragmatic
move. It was not merely about what I could do with a great
group of people backing me up. I was beginning to realize that
becoming an Anglican was rooted in some overarching plan of
God. That was the revelation—that God may be up to some-

thing by matching me with the Anglican Church. I am used to being practical, and so I was left wondering what that bigger idea and plan might be.

## DULY ORDAINED

As conversations with Bishop Murphy and other Anglican Mission leaders progressed, it was proposed that I should be ordained a deacon and then, after the appointed waiting period, a priest. Silly me, I thought I was already ordained. Evidently a certificate signed in a back office that mistakenly left off the year doesn't count in come circles. Who knew?

What exactly is ordination? From my perspective it means that God sets someone in a place of service, in an office, role or order. In the more liturgical world of Catholics, the Orthodox and Anglicans, as well as in many Protestant denominations, the definition of ordination is consistent, but the practices associated with ordination are varied. In my Calvary Chapel and Vineyard days we endeavored to maximize our connection to the whole body and minimize places of special honor. Because we believed in the calling of *all* women and men in the church, and seeking to be pragmatic and humble, not ceremonious, we did not emphasize the ordination of church leaders. I never went through an ordination service in Calvary Chapel or the Vineyard. The certificate was mailed to me because I needed it for a practical reason: to get into hospitals to pray for the sick. Of course I would later need the ordination certificate to officiate at weddings, but at the time I just needed a hall pass to pray without hassle from security.

Do low-church leaders lack respect for the calling of God and thus fail to memorialize ordination in a formal ceremony? Do high-church leaders lack the humility of service the low-church leaders value? Neither is a fair criticism. Each just highlights one side of a coin. The low churches rightly emphasize that all are servants, and that ordained people are servants set aside for a certain task. But no liturgical leader would deny that! In addition, they choose to highlight God's call to ministry with a formal recognition in a prescribed worship service.

Because I had all the compulsory theological education and long years of pastoral and bishop-like experience, after completing a few mandatory courses in Anglican studies, I was ready to graduate from a mere functional ordination to "Holy Orders," which refers to ordination to three orders in the church, *deacon*—an ordained servant usually ministering in a local church, *priest*—the minister ordained to conduct sacramental worship, and *bishop*—the overseer of churches and priests, usually in a district called a diocese.

## ORDAINED A DEACON

I was first ordained to the diaconate. No one in the Anglican Mission likes to tell this story, but I am not sure why. If Jesus could be born in a stable to a virgin, surely a fly-in bishop, working the room of the chapel of an airport in Houston, could ordain me a servant. Let's just say that my ordination to the diaconate, October 25, 2008, was *special* in just this humble sort of way. Here is how it unfolded.

I travel a good deal. My brother bishops in the Anglican Mission travel a good deal too. This made it hard for us to get together for a proper church-based ordination service. As we checked schedules, we noted that I was to be in Houston in late October for a speaking engagement. My colleague Bishop Philip Jones lived at the time, in Little Rock. I don't know if Bishop Jones drew the short straw at a Council of Bishops meeting, or if the bishops simply figured he lived closest to Houston, or if from his delightful temperament and generous spirit he simply offered to come. Whatever the case, Bishop Jones made arrangements with the chaplain to use the chapel at George Bush Intercontinental Airport in Houston.

After my speaking engagement I met Bishop Jones and a rector from a local Anglican church at the terminal. The three of us had to wait for the chaplain to escort us through security so we could get to the chapel and to Holy Orders.

We were on a tight schedule and the chaplain was running late. After some delay, the chaplain finally arrived and walked us through security. Given the ticking clock, we moved quickly to the chapel, a little room with a couple of pews, a table and a small lectern, but not a religious symbol of any kind to be found. The lack of decoration must have been a budget decision or a designer's nod to pluralism. There were no windows either. Okay, no problem so far; still not as controversial as "no room in the inn."

Bishop Jones, unlike me, knew exactly what he was doing. He cheerfully but reverently led us through a brief service that began with my friend Reverend Ron McCrary, who met us at the airport, presenting me. We then read Scripture and heard a few brief comments from Bishop Jones.

I was then *examined*. (It didn't hurt. No medical tools came into play.) Though the circumstances were unusual, and the scene and surrounding events humorous, I, like everyone else in the room, took my examination and vows very seriously. We confessed together that all present understood the importance of the role and responsibilities of deacons. Among other things,

I promised to be a servant to the church, to look for Christ in all others, to study and follow the Scriptures, and to be a model of service in my life and among those with whom I work.

As peculiar as this setting was, the experience of *ordination* was real. It is more than just a traditional rite to me: With God's help, I plan to always be a deacon, to never graduate from being a servant, to be "modest, humble, strong and constant," as the Book of Common Prayer says.

A consecration prayer was said over me, hands were laid on me, I was vested with a deacon's stole and given a beautiful Bible to remind me of the story out of which all this flows—both the funny and the solemn bits. After Eucharist and a closing blessing, we were out the door, leaving the chapel to the guy in the back looking for a place to nap.

Ron had to catch a flight, but Bishop Jones, the woman who drove me to the airport, the local rector and I took the chaplain to get some coffee. He said he'd never seen anything like that service. That made two of us. After some delightful conversation I was on my way again, stole and Bible in hand. I found myself desiring more than ever to announce, embody and demonstrate the words and works of Jesus. I did feel more like a servant—and was glad to be God's deacon.

## ORDAINED A PRIEST

My ordination to the priesthood was highly regular. It took place at St. James Anglican Church in Newport Beach, California. I think of St. James as a sister church—an older and wiser sister—to my new church in Costa Mesa. The rector, Richard Crocker, and assisting priest, Cathie Young, warmly welcomed us to the neighborhood and have been a great support.

I was honored to have Dallas Willard to preach at the ordination service. Many of my new friends from the Anglican Mission attended, as did my extended family and friends from every era of my life: Calvary Chapel, the Vineyard, the independent/alternative church years and Alpha USA.

Now that I was a priest, I was faced with a most cherished, weighty and profound duty: to lead a congregation in the Eucharist. As the caddie said to golfer Francis Ouimet, the 1913 U.S. Open champion, in the movie *The Greatest Game Ever Played*, leading communion "was easy-peasy, lemon-squeezy" in my low-church background. But the rumbles in my belly told me that leading Holy Eucharist was going to be like hitting the first tee shot in front of a crowd at the Masters—when you've never swung a golf club in your life!

# 8

# Giving and Receiving
# the Eucharist

In January of 2009 I attended my first Anglican Mission winter conference. Because I was giving a plenary talk, I went to check on the room where I would speak, as is my custom. It was a typical cavernous auditorium. There were about fifteen hundred chairs set up in neat rows with appropriately placed aisles. I went up on the stage to get a quick feeling for the space, and then started heading out.

Looking up I noticed a man about to give me a cheerful greeting. It was Clark Lowenfield, an Anglican rector who sees that every aspect of a worship service is done as well and worshipful as possible. After a quick greeting he said, "Would you like to assist with Eucharist tonight?"

I immediately felt like a dozen butterflies were having a Cinco de Mayo dance around a pole in my belly. Clark may not have remembered that I was just a rookie. But I knew I was apt to do something wrong in front of everyone and embarrass Bishop

Chuck. In my heart I said, *No way!* I think I said something more appropriate and dignified to Clark.

When Clark rolled his eyes, probably thinking, *They don't make deacons like they used to,* I took it as my sign to get out of there and hide in my hotel room before I got exposed.

### EUCHARISTIC ANXIETY

If anyone could have seen into my anxious heart, known my fearful mind or experienced my anxiety-ridden body the first time I had to celebrate Eucharist, they'd have recognized that I sometimes battle with others' perceptions of me.

I have been speaking and leading in very public roles for thirty-some years. I rarely get nervous. Public speaking for me is like walking or drinking water. Usually I don't even think about it. But the idea of my first public celebration of Eucharist was getting to me.

At this time I was preparing to lead my first Anglican church plant, Holy Trinity Anglican Church in Costa Mesa in their first Sunday worship liturgy. I thought about it and actually dreaded it for weeks before.

In one particularly vulnerable moment of self-reflection, I thought I heard the voice of God whisper in my heart: "Todd, I did not give you and your fellow Jesus followers this sacramental meal to make you so nervous that you can't even be alert to my presence." I'm not sure God ever uses the word *relax,* but something like that is the message I received from him. And I did—I calmed down, chilled out and lightened up about 85 percent after receiving God's good news regarding Eucharist.

I know I will always take celebrating the Eucharist seriously. I hope to never get over the awe and reverence. But those things are different than self-focused, self-absorbed fear. After a few months of celebrating Eucharist with my congregation, I am able to be more present and less self-conscious.

## EUCHARISTIC WINE

I don't drink. In fact I don't like the taste of alcohol in any of its forms. I can't even stand the *smell* of beer. Hard liquor in my book is just flat crazy. It tastes like poison. Wine may be the most bizarre to me. For the life of me, I can't figure out why people would want to drink something with their dinner that tastes like cough syrup, which in my opinion doesn't pair well with anything.

Why is my distaste for alcohol relevant? Because the Anglican tradition celebrates Eucharist weekly. And the proper way to care for leftover wine from Holy Eucharist is to either drink it or pour it directly back into the earth. Not on a bush, shrub or grass, but onto the ground. Some churches even have a *piscina*— a basin which has a pipe hooked to it that goes directly into the ground. Being a church plant, we don't have that available to us. All we can do is reverently drink the wine.

Our first Sunday Eucharist as a church plant was beautiful and spiritually nourishing. I typically get to church at 7 or 7:30 to finish setting up for the service, and I don't like to eat that early in the morning. I never drink coffee and don't drink tea that early either. So when Eucharist was over and we were tearing down after church, a couple of our leaders and I stood around the altar table with a "What do we do now?" look on our faces.

Knowing this was a time to be a strong and decisive leader, I boldly picked up one of the chalices and began to do my best to drink the wine reverently. Almost immediately my face flushed and my ears turned red and hot. Not that I was even slightly inebriated, but I did wonder if I was going to pass out. I'll never do that again! We have found different worshipful ways to care for the leftover wine that don't flush the face of the priest.

### THE MEANING AND POWER OF EUCHARIST

Why is a kiss almost always more than *just* a kiss? As the Temptations sang, "If you wanna know / If he loves you so / It's in his kiss." Kisses signify things like love, romance, joy, concern or even hello or goodbye. Kisses also impart affection, communicate warmth, and disclose our truest inner feelings and the value we place on someone.

Eucharist is like this. It conveys the love and purpose of God for his people. Consecrated and consumed bread and wine are never *just* the cells of wheat and grapes touching our lips. Jesus *disclosed* himself to his first followers in the breaking of bread. The confused disciples of the first Easter did not recognize Jesus in the gait of his walk or by the character of his voice. They failed to discern his presence in his teaching of the Scriptures. But when Jesus gave thanks, broke the bread and gave it them, their eyes were opened and they recognized him.

Clarity of God's love and intention for us is mediated to us in the broken body and shed blood of Jesus. In the Eucharist we, though steeped in the concrete reality of space and time, connect with a reality that transcends grain and grape. When we receive the Eucharist, we are united with Jesus' past—his death and resurrection. We are also simultaneously joined to God's future—the consummation of all things in the new heaven and the new earth.

These twin realities nourish us in deeply spiritual ways. We have a word for this, *mystery*. Not mystery in the sense of obscurity or ambiguity, but in the sense of transcendence, of something that wildly exceeds our capacity to fully understand—like the mystery of a kiss. How do united lips produce a lifelong commitment of "for better, for worse, for richer, for poorer"? On one level I do not know. It is a mystery. But on another level I have deep understanding. I have more than thirty years of loving and being loved through kisses from my wife.

Presently my congregation and I are embarking on a similar journey. Having said to Jesus that we will follow in riches, poverty, good times and bad, he is communicated to us in Spirit power through the breaking of bread and drinking of wine. As deep love is born in a simple first kiss, celebrating the Eucharist similarly changes us. We find deeper levels of forgiveness and freedom. In that freedom we discover that the spiritual nourishment we receive is not just for our own sake but for the sake of others.

## BECOMING THE ACCIDENTAL BISHOP

By the time I was ordained a priest, some had already suggested that, in order to take on the work of planting two hundred new Anglican churches on the West Coast, God might be calling me to be a bishop. I should have known it was futile to refuse—especially if my reticence was based on doing life *my* way.

# 9

# Consecrated as a Bishop

A *bishop* is the spiritual overseer of churches and their pastors. I resisted the thought of being a bishop. I was still being tempted to flee responsibility in favor of semiretirement. And *overseer,* as I knew from experience, is spelled r-e-s-p-o-n-s-i-b-i-l-i-t-y! But in his gracious, Southern, "I don't take no for an answer" way, Bishop Murphy insisted that it would be important for me to have authority commensurate with my responsibilities as a church planter on the West Coast.

From an episcopal oversight point of view, I could see Bishop Murphy's reasoning. But I also realized that, as much as Bishop Murphy and I were getting to know each other and developing a warm friendship, our imaginations for ministry were shaped and influenced by very different histories and mentors. Bishop Murphy, in my mind, is a proper bishop with all the right experiences. Coming from a low-church background, I felt I was neither ready nor suited to be a bishop.

Part of the problem was that I lacked imagination. I have known and been influenced by pastors who planted churches:

most notably Chuck Smith, founder of the Calvary Chapel movement, and John Wimber, leader of Vineyard Churches. Presbyterian pastor Tim Keller, based in New York City, is possibly today's best-known example. But, revealing my obvious ignorance, I'd never known a bishop who planted churches. Later I learned that there have, of course, been bishops who planted churches—starting with the apostle Paul, to Saint Patrick, to my new heroes, Archbishop Emmanuel Kolini and Bishop John Rucyahana. But at the time I kept saying to Bishop Murphy, "I don't need to be a bishop. As the former president of the Vineyard, I've already done bishop-type work—even overseeing other bishop types. Look at Chuck Smith, John Wimber and Tim Keller," I argued, "they are *just* pastors, and they do perfectly fine planting churches."

Nevertheless, Bishop Chuck and the Holy Spirit convinced me that being consecrated as a bishop was the right and responsible thing to do. *Right* because it was responding to God's call. *Responsible* because birthing churches means raising them too, not abandoning them to the forces of an increasingly hostile culture.

## THE MISSING CROSS

Six months later I was about to be consecrated as a bishop. All the bishops and archbishops were standing in a room behind the sanctuary, greeting one another and waiting for the consecration preacher, Rick Warren, to arrive. As Rick was putting the wireless microphone on, I noticed that all the other bishops had large crosses hanging from their necks. These pectoral crosses symbolize that the wearer is a member of the clergy.

There must have been some Spirit-led discernment happening in the room because just at that moment my beloved archbishop, Emmanuel Kolini of Rwanda, asked where my cross was. The Rwandans are not big on religious decorations, but even His Grace had on a traditional pectoral cross, as is customary for Rwandan bishops. I said that I didn't have one. Like a younger brother ratting out his big brother to Dad, I was tempted to blame Bishop Murphy but thought better of it. Archbishop Kolini replied that I should have one.

I can't remember if my friend Bishop Sandy Greene overheard what was being said, or if I asked him what to do about my less-than-ideal pectoral problem, but he came to the rescue in a most graceful and loving way. He took off his pectoral cross, which had been given to him at his consecration, and gave it to me, saying "I have an extra one."

After the service was over I approached Sandy to give him his cross back. Sandy said, "No, it is yours."

"To keep?" I asked.

"Yes," he replied. "The Lord spoke to me during Rick's sermon. It is yours to keep."

I keep it in a safe and treasured place. It is pure silver with eleven handsome amethyst stones—perhaps emblematic of the eleven faithful disciples. Every time I put it on I think of the humility, grace and generosity of those faithful apostles and bishops who have gone before me. In these moments I know something is going on that is decidedly not accidental.

### A Bishop with a Collar but No Ring

My public life as a bishop got off to a challenging start. It was early on a Saturday morning and I was getting dressed in the cramped quarters of the bathroom in our hotel room. I was dressing in full clergy wear, collar and all, for the consecration service of a friend as a bishop. It felt like I was in Little League again. I loved putting on uniforms when I was a kid. It was a big day, and out of respect I wanted to look nice. I also had a working-lunch meeting afterward with three colleagues.

As I was putting on my collar, which is still not an easy task for me, I looked at Debbie, sitting on the side of the bed, and said to her, "Great! The first time I am going to wear my collar in public and it is October 31st—Halloween. Everyone will think I'm wearing a costume." Such, I guess, is the fate of an accidental bishop.

I walked out the door into the California sun thinking I didn't look too bad in purple. I was ready and happy to meet the challenges of the day—the toughest thing to brave, I thought, would be an extraordinarily long church service. But things got stickier than that pretty much right away. Upon arrival at the church I was guided into a room reserved so the bishops could robe in private.

Have you ever been in a room with dignitaries of some sort and known right away you were out of your league—no matter how kind everyone was being? In fact, you are sure that the kindness is a polite cover for what they are all thinking: *What is he doing here?* Remember the terrifying days of junior high school when you had to shower after PE? That was me.

I thought, sometimes even feared, that someday I would be exposed as not just accidental but as an *imposter.* I never dreamed it would come at my first public outing as a bishop.

All the guys around me were putting on these amazing copes and miters. Who knew grown, gray-haired and balding men could be *lookers* in embroidered gowns?

I should interject here that I have no issue with high-church accoutrements. I have great respect for all the Anglo-Catholics I have met so far. But coming from a low-church background, the high-church trappings made me feel like an awkward, self-conscious kid at his first formal dance.

Just when I was getting over the envy of not having a cope and miter—and thank God for my brother bishop from Africa in the room, because he didn't wear them either—I noticed two beautiful certificates lying on a nearby table. They looked like pieces of fine art.

I next noticed a man and woman standing behind a desk. The woman was holding up what appeared to be an electric glue gun to see if the tube of stuff loaded in the gun was melting. As it turned out, the glue gun had wax in it, and the woman began putting small dollops of melted wax on the edges of the certificates. Then, one by one the bishops approached the table. After signing their names they took their enormous rings from their hands and sealed their signature in wax. This is an ancient and serious practice. The ecclesiastical rings worn by bishops are used to seal solemn documents, signifying that the bishop is acting in fidelity with and on behalf of the church.

I again felt exceptionally *accidental.* It was like one of those recurring dreams that athletes have when it is time to perform but they left their uniform at home. What was I to do? I have no Super Bowl Championship–like ring to seal my signature. But what I lack in ecclesiastical sophistication, I make up for with creativity. Searching my hands, I noticed my wedding ring. It is a golden circle of intertwined leaves with a distinctive cross in the middle. It has not been off my hand many times in thirty-three years, but this was a moment I needed it to come off and come through for me.

Happily I had been losing weight, so there was a small chance I could get if off. Seeing that there were several more coped and mitered bishops ahead of me, I coughed nervously and excused myself. I made my way to the bridal room next door looking for a sink with a soap dispenser and some running water, only to run into the pacing bishop-elect. Turning on my heels, I went for it in the hallway. In full public view I licked my ring finger and pulled on the ring just hard enough to avoid knuckle surgery. The ring came off, and I wandered back into the room, trying to look nonchalant.

After the next to last guy signed and sealed the document, I did the same with my wedding ring. Thanks be to God, no one seemed to notice. Or maybe they thought I came from a poor diocese and could only afford small jewelry. I don't know.

If anyone ever asks me about this, I've got an explanation: my seal is symbolic. The meaning of the cross is obvious. The leaves stand for life and growth. So my seal is nothing to blush about, it signifies the life of the cross. None of those Super Bowl rings can top that.

## YOU CAN'T TAKE ME ANYWHERE

Thinking I had conquered the day's biggest challenge, feeling wise and a little more bishopy, I began to mill around with the other Holy Order folks on the patio outside the church. It seemed like the safest place to stay out of awkward moments or even flat-out trouble. Right. As the procession began to make it's way into the narthex, I fell in line and walked with the lone black bishop from Africa. Just before we were to sing the processional, I said to him, "Look at us. Two African bishops processing side by side into church." I am enormously fond of and proud of my canonical connection to Rwanda.

The way he looked at me reminded me of an old joke: A flea and an elephant walked over a rickety rope-and-slat bridge. As they got to the other side, the flea looked up at the elephant and exclaimed, "Boy, did we shake that thing." My brother bishop looked at me as if I'd just said to him, "Boy, are we African!" He supplied all the black and 99 percent of the African. I was the accidental flea.

The rest of the processional went off without the smallest hitch. We clergy and bishops took the places assigned to us at the rehearsal the night before. Everything was going well. When I got confused about what to do, I just kept my eye on the veteran bishops with the big rings.

Unfortunately, at that time I was struggling with asthma, and the deacon swinging the thurible, a golden censer of incense, was only about three feet away from me. The inflammation in my airways was causing wheezing, shortness of breath and tightness in my chest.

I had been warned about making sure to use the toilet *before* putting on my vestments, but no one warned me to stay a certain distance from the thurifer (the deacon who swings the thurible) or risk possible suffocation at my first consecration. All of the other clergy looked completely at peace, taking it all in with joy. I told myself to hang in there: fresh Newport Beach air and lunch with the boys was not far off.

The service ended. My friend Bill Thompson was consecrated bishop. While he greeted friends, family and colleagues in the narthex, I headed for the antechamber to find a box of tissues and take my bishop garb off. Longing for the fresh, cool, outdoor air, I said quick goodbyes and hustled out to the patio to meet my lunch companions. We quickly agreed to eat at a Mexican place and headed off. As we arrived, I learned that I have the gift of prophecy.

### HALLOWEEN DAY IN A COLLAR

Three of us, being Anglican clergy, had collars on. My friend Keith, a non-Anglican pastor, had no collar but was smartly dressed. I stood out in particular because of my purple shirt. The Reverends Tony Baron and Ellis Brust were wearing black. As we walked into the busy lunchtime scene, every eye in the place turned to look at us. Befuddled, I didn't get what was going on.

But in the next instant I noticed that all the servers were dressed up in Halloween costumes. Having some business to do, we asked for a quiet corner table. As we made our way over to it, all eyes followed us. I think they were taking bets as to whether we were in costume.

We settled into our seats, and our server—a girl in a Wonder Woman costume—quickly arrived. Surveying her new customers, she blurted out, "Are you guys real priests?"

See? I am a *prophet*. I knew it! The first time I wear my collar in public, its Halloween and I get carded. Just a day in the life of the accidental bishop.

### HOLY ORDERS

Beyond being an amusing story, I think there is something more to it. For most of my past my colleagues and I made as little fuss as possible about being pastors. We were proud of wearing our California surf wear. We liked to be cool and tried to blend in with our culture. I am not saying that is wrong, but wearing a purple shirt and white collar has its advantages.

My new clothing makes me take my call to ministry more seriously. Not just the functions of preaching, leading and doing spiritual formation, but the call to be a model of Christlikeness. And that is a high calling today when clergy are more apt to be ridiculed than respected.

Why did God take me through the process of Holy Orders in such a unique fashion? I think he was giving this low-church boy a firm and stable bridge to cross over into a new world. I am glad to be here, and it is wonderful to be able to serve in this way. (Though I still feel a little awkward in a collar.)

While some elements of the Anglican tradition (vestments and procedures) make me uncomfortably self-conscious, I otherwise feel right at home. In part two I will share some of my favorite parts of Anglicanism.

# PART TWO

# What I Like About
# Anglicanism

# 10

# A Story to Embody

*N. T. Wright*

Over the past decade or so I have been reviewing my sense of what it means to be a Christian. As I've done so, I've seen more clearly the story that gives meaning to all my roles in life: husband, father, friend and missionary bishop. N. T. Wright has helped me do this.

What does it mean to be a Christian? One way to get at the answer is to rephrase it: for what purpose was the church called into being? N. T. Wright says:

> According to the early Christians, the church doesn't exist in order to provide a place where people can pursue their private spiritual agendas and develop their own spiritual potential. Nor does it exist in order to provide a safe haven in which people can hide from the wicked world and ensure that they themselves arrive safely at an otherworldly destination. Private spiritual growth and ultimate salva-

tion come rather as the byproduct of the main, central overarching purpose for which God has called and is calling us. . . . [T]hat through the church God will announce to the world that he is indeed its wise, loving and just creator; that through Jesus he has defeated the powers that corrupt and enslave it; and that by his Spirit he is at work to heal and renew it.

This biblical narrative has been the massive Wrightian corrective of the last part of my life. And in this case I did know that Tom Wright is an Anglican—not even a low-church evangelical like me could miss that! Let me explain now how Wright's work has given new contour to my faith.

I have been trying to follow Jesus for a long time and have seriously read and studied the Bible. My background provided me lenses through which to read the Scriptures, and I had read them with an open mind and with all the intellect and devotion I had. Thus I knew lots of Bible facts, studied various theologies and followed doctrinal debates. But somehow, along the way, I lost the foundational story of the Bible. This is no small thing. When we lose sight of the overall narrative of the Bible, we are left knowing what to think but not how to live.

Once we see that our doctrines and systematic theologies come from a story, that story invites us to dwell within it. Humans were created to live in God's story. But over the centuries we have written alternative stories for ourselves. There are stories of power and passion, of lust and greed, of anger, manipulation and retribution. To varying degrees, these narratives are inescapable and control virtually everyone.

But the Bible gives us the narrative of freedom that most of us long for deep inside. It tells us a story that invites our participation. Hearing the story of the Bible is not like hearing about the latest hit on Broadway. It's like getting a call from the director asking us to take a part in the drama.

The kingdom of God is the ultimate drama. No drug or sex or food or prized possession begins to compare! Those who work with God through the power of the Holy Spirit to rescue the enslaved, to find lost souls, to create culture or to seek justice find life, the rich life God intended for all humanity.

For me, discovering the works of Wright has been paradigm shifting. Wright unveils the truth that being a Christian is more—much more—than "going to heaven when I die." Understanding and indwelling the biblical narrative provides the context for doing works of goodness and justice without having to worry whether works are meritorious (of course they aren't). It fires the imagination, and impels us toward spiritual formation.

No one has influenced my overall theology more in the last decade than Tom Wright. Thus, when called to the Anglican Church, I knew I had found someone who could be my lifelong teacher.

### MEET N. T. WRIGHT

N. T. Wright is the former bishop of Durham in the Church of England, and is presently professor of New Testament at the University of St. Andrews. He is a highly respected New Testament scholar and author of over thirty books. He came to prominence in the American evangelical world through his orthodox interactions with and challenges to the scholars of the Jesus Seminar. Among laypeople, he is better known for *Surprised by Hope* and *The Challenge of Jesus*.

### FINDING A BIGGER STORY AND COMPREHENSIVE JESUS

Wright has ongoing influence in my work as a missionary bishop because he helps me be more than a mere Christian, pastor or bishop—he points the way to being a Christ follower in the kingdom of God. The first time I read Wright's discussion of "the aims of Jesus," I remember thinking, *Can't this be said in a sentence or a paragraph? Others are satisfied with the notion that Jesus' aim was singular: to die for the sins of the world so that we can go to heaven. What more is there to be said?* According to Wright, a lot.

Jesus was born of a virgin within a specific time and place in history. He did not drop out of the blue sky on a golden chariot. The Pharisees, Sadducees, Herodians, Zealots and Essenes are not just trivial bits of background. They matter. They represent, to one degree or another, wrong ways of thinking about what it means to be the people of God. They misunderstand the aims of God in Christ.

Jesus' parables are not just pithy and powerful moral lessons. They are windows into another world. They unveil the aims of Jesus and his gospel of the kingdom. For instance, the parable of the good Samaritan is not just a nice Sunday school lesson to teach kids to be generous to those in need. It's a powerful lesson about what God is up to in and through his people. The parable teaches us that love—the God-inspired will to do good to others—trumps religion.

The priest and the Levite could not risk, according to their religion, touching or even getting too near a corpse. Jesus teaches us that in doing the right religious thing they did the wrong kingdom thing. Within the worldview of *the aims of Jesus*, that beaten-half-dead man (whether or not he was a member of their tribe) was their neighbor. This teaches us a fundamental truth about the aims of Jesus: God, and thus Jesus, is in solidarity with his broken creation. Jesus' followers are to be too.

The words and works of Jesus set forth his aims. They are chiefly concerned with restoring humanity to its God-intended role in this world and the world to come. Put a different way, Jesus embodies his aims. He is Adam and Eve, Israel and the church as God intended. Jesus' aims and work through the Spirit have to do with restoring, reconstituting and resending the people of God. Forgiveness of sins is of course central to these aims, but the aims of Jesus cannot be reduced to mere forgiveness.

Sin and forgiveness arise from within a story. They have no real meaning apart from that story. Jesus, coming to earth within the story of God—creation, fall, Israel, redemption, church—takes his aims from that story.

Thus Jesus' pattern of life, his announcing, embodying and demonstrating the gospel of the kingdom, clearly set out his chief aim—to create a people who partner with God in putting the world to rights. This of course includes dealing with personal sin through forgiveness and freedom. It includes reconciling us to our God and Maker, whom we have offended. Life in Jesus is regenerating, giving his followers a different kind of life both now and in the eschaton. Thus Jesus' aims include taking care of our life in the world to come. But crucially, the message of the kingdom, the proclamation that best explains the aims of Jesus, orients us to this life, and especially to the least, the last, the left out and the broken.

Jesus was very self-conscious of his Father-derived aims. An incident in the Upper Room makes this clear. What would you do if you knew that God had called you and given you favor? Jesus' example provides the answer:

Jesus knew that the Father had put him in complete charge of everything, that he came from God and was on his way back to God. So he got up from the supper table, set aside his robe, and put on an apron. Then he poured water into a basin and began to wash the feet of the disciples, drying them with his apron. (John 13:3-5)

Jesus expressed his aims in this story. He gave us a living picture of "the Son of Man did not come to be served, but to serve, and to give his life as a ransom" (Matthew 20:28 NIV). He modeled for us what it means to be the reconstituted people of God through his forgiveness and the power of the Holy Spirit. Knowing his place in the world, he did not demand favor or privilege from others, rather he performed menial service. For two millennia this tedious and basic work has been the model for kingdom-based change agents all over the world. People of every nation, language and ethnicity have been inspired by this story to enter the story of God as the cooperative friends of Jesus, seeking to live like their Master in creative goodness through the power of the Holy Spirit.

#### JOURNEY INWARD, JOURNEY OUTWARD

Anglicanism at its best has always been marked by a twin journey: *inward* into the story of God as revealed in the Scriptures, and *outward* as we announce and embody the story in the world. These dual foci bring into play both personal piety and service to others.

Among Wright's many gifts to the church is his insistence that the story the lectionary readings tell us is *our* story—and that our biblically derived story is personal and public, interior and civic.

I am experiencing this firsthand as I begin to teach weekly Bible studies (i.e., preach sermons) based on the lectionary readings during Sunday services. As we study, we ask ourselves two Wright-based questions: (1) what is the story that is being told, and (2) what is our part to play in this ongoing story?

These two questions put us squarely in line with the intent of the English Reformers. They were not just trying to reform the church as an institution; they sought to reform the church conceived of as a community of followers of Jesus. They, rightly in my view, concluded that as a part of our common liturgy, telling the story of the Bible every year through the reading of the lectionary would shape the inner and outer reality of both individuals and the church.

Our Anglican forefathers were right. It is true. Telling ourselves the biblical story through the regular preaching of the Word has a powerful shaping influence. I am forever grateful to Tom Wright for resolutely putting story above disembodied bits of theology, for giving the church a story to live, not just proper thoughts to think.

Once we begin to follow Jesus in this manner, we enter the story he was telling, we receive the good news he was proclaiming—the gospel of the kingdom of God. In chapter ten we will look at how the church is created and sustained by the power of the kingdom of God at work in our world.

# II

# Anglicanism and the Kingdom of God

While Anglicans have a very high view of the church, Anglicanism at its best is not self-conscious. It is kingdom conscious. I first learned this by tagging along with John Wimber as he interacted with Anglican friends like Reverend David Watson, Bishop David Pytches and Bishop Sandy Millar. There was never a doubt that these leaders were Anglican. But that is not what they wore on their sleeves. Echoing their hearts, their sleeves read, "The gospel of the kingdom of God."

This was important for me because before I could become an Anglican, I had to answer a more fundamental question: Was I sure Anglican churches were more kingdom-focused than church-centered?

### Putting the Church in It's Place

The best thing that could happen to any church is that it be "put in its place." This is critically important to me. Likening the church to a seed, it cannot grow sitting in its packaging. The seed must be placed in the ground of the kingdom, lose its life there, and then flourish and grow as a product and agent of the kingdom. That is, the kingdom of God creates the church. Thus the church is derivative and secondary. Therefore the kingdom—the rule and reign, or the expression or action—of God is our highest priority. Misunderstanding this has been the root cause of innumerable troubles and failures in churches of all denominations. I needed assurance that the Anglican world could keep the logic straight. Knowing Wimber's colleagues— Watson, Pytches and Millar, most notably—assured me that in the Anglican Church I could be in alignment with the following agenda: the kingdom first, the catholic (universal) church second, and the various brands of church third.

This agenda is not born of the desire to be free of ecclesiastical authority. I am not looking for freedom from the church. I am looking to be bound to the kingdom of God. It's best not to try to think from the institutional forms of the church outward, but from the gospel of the kingdom and the mission field backward. I like what Matthew 5:48 says: "You're kingdom subjects. Now live like it. Live out your God-created identity. Live generously and graciously toward others, the way God lives toward you."

Once we get God's purpose and mission for the church right, it informs our ecclesiology—gives meaning and shape to the church. As noted missiologist David Bosch says, "Mission is not so much an activity of the Church, but an attribute of God. There is a Church because there is a mission." Or as an Anglican scholar has put it, "The task of the church is defined for it. It is the herald and foretaste of the Kingdom of God."

Putting the kingdom of God first is crucial for many reasons, but not the least this: in our age the church is not thought well of. Some sociologists even think that that the church is at risk of complete failure. Dallas Willard has a far better perspective: "The kingdom of God is never at risk." And since the kingdom creates and sustains the church, the church is never at risk either.

This knowledge and the confidence that flows from it allows the church to follow Jesus and his kingdom agenda into the world. Like the King, we can stay in solidarity with the world he created. We don't have to flee the world to pursue an alleged righteousness that is in fact far from God, who always stays with his broken creation. One of the things I like most about the Anglican Church is that it is able to completely differentiate itself from the world as a Christian church while simultaneously being in and connected to the world.

This gave me confidence as I considered joining the Anglican Mission. I needed to know that the Anglican Mission was not coming into being against the backdrop of the ecclesiastical trouble within the Anglican world, but rather within the larger narrative of God: his choosing and sending a people to live in alignment with the aims of Jesus through the ministry of the Holy Spirit. I happily found the latter to be the case.

For the last ten years or so, due to the good work of the missional church movement, many denominations have been rethinking ecclesiology (what it means to be the church). Vast parts of the worldwide Anglican Communion have been at the front of this. This is true of Archbishop Kolini and the church he shepherds, the Anglican Church in Rwanda, which birthed the Anglican Mission. And of course the Anglican Mission gave birth to my work on the West Coast, Churches for the Sake of Others.

### FOR ALL LEADERS

A leadership truism says that once the leadership decides what to measure and celebrate within an enterprise, they will have set the corporate culture of the enterprise. By choosing what counts, we cement into place the ethos, spirit and Zeitgeist of businesses, schools and churches. This is both a great challenge and a great opportunity.

Make your measurements kingdom-based—make your celebrations missional. I came to see that I would not only have permission to create and lead missional churches in the Anglican Mission, but that such a decision would be celebrated as the correct course of action.

The big test now lies ahead of me: will Holy Trinity Anglican Church in Costa Mesa, California, embody kingdom values? Or will we fall prey to the common trap of having *notional* versus *real* values? There is only one faultless way for any church to know this: examine how we spend our time, money and energy; check our calendar (time and energy) and test our budget and checkbook (money). These will be our prophets, like having Isaiah and Amos at our leadership meetings. They will lead us where the church is supposed to be: at the intersection of real life making known life in the kingdom. We call this evangelism.

# 12

# The Anglican
# Evangelistic Tradition

Evangelistic church planting, which is my enterprise, is not easy. If it were, more people would attempt it. Since I was a little kid, I have had the unfortunate reputation of not being smart enough to avoid hard things. Being a veteran pastor and church planter would suggest that I could at least pull off a basic introductory first meeting. Not necessarily.

In 2009 I attempted insanity—or at least that is what some people tell me. I started two churches simultaneously, in Costa Mesa, California, and Eagle, Idaho. I'll never forget the first meeting of the church plant in Eagle. Right from the beginning I wanted to connect spiritual formation through liturgy with mission in the world. Thus for that first night, in addition to singing a couple of songs, I prepared a short vision-casting talk and a compline for closing prayer. A compline is an evening rite of prayer used just before bedtime. I think I got the elements for the compline from an online prayer book source. I've been praying for thirty-four years and leading groups in prayer for as long, so I did not think it would be a big deal to lead a group in compline. I thought it would be a good way to put a key value in place right away.

As I was passing out the papers printed with the compline prayers, I remembered some unfamiliar elements on the page that I had intended to Google, but got busy and forgot. On the page was a stanza of about eight lines to pray. Each line of this section started with a *V* or an *R*. There was also an occasional asterisk on the page. I had no clue about the asterisks, but I had determined that the *V* must stand for "vicar" and the *R* for "the *rest* of you." Thus I surmised that I would read the *V* parts and the rest of the group the *R* parts. Fortunately, I am not given to too much pride. Pride doesn't go well with planting churches. Missionary bishops have to be able to take risks and fail.

In our group was a married couple of veteran Episcopalians/ Anglicans who were even experienced members of an Anglican Mission church plant. (Having them there was a great comfort to me.) Thus as I passed out the papers I thought I'd ask them about the *V*s, *R*s and asterisks. They informed me that the asterisks are gentle, literary stop signs that alerted us to *let someone else read.*

Then my friends informed me that the *V* stood for "versicle" and the *R* for "response." The leader read the *V* parts and the others read the *R* parts. I wasn't that far off! Not bad for someone on their way to being an accidental missionary bishop. I was showing some real potential.

### JOHN WESLEY: A HERO AND MODEL

I am not much of a trinket or figurine guy. In fact I have had only one in my whole life: an antique figurine of John Wesley. In all my numerous offices, there has been one constant: John Wesley. He is an icon of a preacher of the gospel: holy and practical, an effective leader, concerned for social justice, lover of evangelism and discipleship. Wesley also loved the church and those outside the church so much that he was willing to stir things up within his church.

In a conversation with J. I. Packer I asked if I could count Wesley as an Anglican, and thus another bit of glass in the mosaic. Or was Wesley owned, so to speak, by the Methodists? Packer answered, emphatically, "Yes, you can count him as an Anglican." Those were just the words I was hoping to hear. All doubts about my fit in the Anglican Church were now banished.

A survey of the life and ministry of John Wesley teaches us that Anglicanism at its best has always been focused on more than right doctrine and correct churchly practice. Throughout its history it has also had a consistent thread of churches and leaders who remained in conversation with those outside the church. Below are six principles that I believe illumine a Wesleyan, evangelistic form of Anglicanism. I recount these principles here not because I think they are exhaustive, but because they are representative. Anglican leaders who embodied these ideas were a big influence in my ability to hear a calling to the Anglican Church. Here, in six quick thoughts, is a Wesleyan-Anglican guide for engaging with those outside the church.

### SIX REPRESENTATIVE PRINCIPLES OF THE ANGLICAN CHURCH

*1. Churches for the sake of others.* While the phrase *churches for the sake of others* is, to my knowledge, mine, the practices behind it surely are not. Over the years, noted English leaders such as the Reverend John Collins and Bishop Sandy Millar, successive rectors at Holy Trinity Brompton in London, inspired me to lead an Anglican church that kept its focus on those without faith. Both these leaders, following in the footsteps of Jesus, stayed in conversation with contemporary seekers. As cultural context and people change, so must church leaders. How does a pastor keep up and change the way she or he communicates in public and private? That takes wisdom, insight and courage. Most don't attempt it.

Harder yet, how does a pastor motivate a church to bend itself to those outside itself, to submit the legitimate institutional concerns to something bigger, to exist for the sake of others? I know of many Anglican rectors who have successfully made these shifts over the past couple decades. To me, Collins and Millar are great representatives of successfully doing this. They are part of the mosaic shaping my life as an Anglican bishop.

**2. Thoughtful and responsive, but not co-opted by culture.** Anglicans have a rich tradition of thinkers on contemporary evangelism. Apologist, evangelist and theologian Michael Green and senior professor of church growth Eddie Gibbs at Fuller Seminary come easily to mind. Green displays what I think of as iconic Anglican intelligence and balance in his more than fifty published books. His *Evangelism Through the Local Church*, though now twenty years old, is still a worthy read for any pastor desiring to reshape their church for the sake of others. And Gibbs has stayed on top of the cultural and generational challenges in evangelism. He is an enlightening and encouraging mentor to hundreds of young leaders. I have turned to him many times for advice and insight. His *ChurchNext* and *Leadership-Next* are good examples of Eddie's capacity to use his intellectual gifts in practical ways.

The Anglican Church also has premier missiologists. Roland
Allen was an Anglican priest and a pioneer missionary from the
late 1890s until the middle of the twentieth century. He is the
author of *Missionary Methods: St. Paul's or Ours?* and *The Spontaneous Expansion of the Church*. His experience led him to a
radical reassessment of the theology and missionary methods of
Western churches. He argued for Paul's practices of discerning
and following the movement of the Holy Spirit in power and
miracles and then adapting the new self-supporting, self-propa-
gating, self-governing churches to their local culture. Though
Allen's ideas had little effect on the churches and missionary
societies of his day, since the 1960s his work has exercised growing influence on missiology and ecclesiology.

Two of the principles I have developed and that shape my
ministry—*engineering churches from the mission field backward*
and *churches for the sake of others*—were born of my lifelong
ruminating on Allen's ideas.

Bishop Lesslie Newbigin is similar to Allen in that he was not
merely a thinker and scholar, but a missionary. For various reasons Bishop Newbigin has lived in my mind as an Anglican for
at least twenty years. I am not alone in counting him as such.
But to be strict about it, while his consecration as a bishop was
recognized by Anglicans, and while he was offered and turned
down an opportunity to be an assistant bishop in the Anglican
Church, he was actually a missionary of the Church of Scotland
and later a bishop in the South Indian United Church. This
church was a union of Presbyterians, Congregationalists, Anglicans and Methodists. In this role he had a profound and
difference-making voice among Anglicans. That is where I came
across him. For instance, I'll never forget a series of talks New-

bigin gave at Holy Trinity Brompton Anglican Church in London not long before he died. He tells the whole story of the Bible in two talks that are simultaneously brilliant and inspiring. I listen to the talks every couple years just to make sure I am keeping my bearings in the story of God.

Much of what is being discussed in contemporary Western missions, in seminaries and in the emerging church movement, is an ongoing comment on Newbigin, and particularly his books *Foolishness to the Greeks* and *The Gospel in a Pluralist Society.* He helps us understand what it means to preach the gospel in a post-Christian culture that is marked not by secularism and no gods, but rather by a paganism that embraces many gods. Newbigin continues to lead the way in helping practitioners think through how to engage the modern and postmodern culture with the gospel.

**3. Power evangelism.** In his generation, perhaps no one embodied evangelism in the Church of England more than David Watson (1933-1984). Under the influence of Dr. Martin Lloyd-Jones, Watson became a prototypical charismatic evangelical. He embodied the best of both traditions. Because both he and John Wimber connected the power of the Spirit to evangelism, it makes sense that they became friends. Along with others, they pioneered what became known as a "third wave" form of evangelism called "power evangelism."

Power evangelism simply expresses the notion that in the New Testament works of power and deeds of healing by Jesus and the apostles usually resulted in persons, families and whole villages coming to faith. Church history bears this out as well. Seeing the practice of power evangelism in the Anglican Church assured me that I would find a home within it.

**4. Evangelism by preaching the Word of God.** Since I have been focusing on English leaders, here I will mention American Anglicans noted for their ability to communicate the Bible with power and clarity: Reverend Terry Fullam, rector of St. Paul's Episcopal Church in Darien, Connecticut; Dr. John Guest of Sewickley, Pennsylvania, a highly regarded Anglican evangelist and pastor; and Reverend Dennis Bennett, best known for his work in renewing the faith of Christians and the life of parishes through the ministry of the Holy Spirit.

Under Terry Fullam's leadership, St. Paul's became one of the most evangelistically effective Episcopal churches in America. Similar to Watson and Wimber, but more directly influenced by Dennis Bennett, Fullam also had a focus on parish renewal. In addition to his gift for communicating, he had a knack for making liturgical worship come alive as a means of evangelism and spiritual formation. I've been told by those who knew him well that probably no person in the last generation of American Episcopalian pastors has helped as many Episcopalians' faith come alive as Terry.

As a young man John Guest was deeply influenced by Billy Graham, and in my mind you could not have a better influence. Because I linked him to Graham, it literally never crossed my mind that Guest was an Episcopalian pastor. As a young man I heard him speak a couple times and, seeking to be a better evangelistic preacher, I used to study his sermons. In retrospect, John represents a few more pieces of glass that have turned into the mosaic of me as a missionary Anglican bishop. As with others, when I close my eyes and imagine a ministry like Fullam's and Guest's, I know that Anglicanism is a place I can thrive, a place where better and more gifted men than I have served with distinction.

**5. Evangelism in a worldwide dialogue.** Agreed upon Anglican tradition says that the gospel, in continuity with its historic proclamations, must be articulated afresh "for the times," for each generation. No one has done this better than Reverend Nicky Gumbel and the worldwide spread of the Alpha Course under his leadership. Nicky, a former barrister, is now, following Sandy Millar, the rector of Holy Trinity Brompton in London.

The Alpha Course began in the 1980s and was consistently nurtured under the watchful and value-shaping eye of Sandy Millar. Nicky Gumbel took over running Alpha at Holy Trinity Brompton in the fall of 1990. Gumbel soon realized that the course had evangelistic potential for those outside the church. Over a period of a few years, Nicky, using his keen mind and practical experience, adjusted the course to fit the conversation of those outside the church.

I don't know of any approach to conversing with seekers that has done more for the cause of Christ than Alpha. In early 2010, the Alpha Course is being run in all fifty U.S. states. Two million Americans have attended Alpha courses over the last decade or so. Worldwide thirteen million people have attended an Alpha course in 163 countries. Perhaps as many as three million or more of these have found faith in Jesus.

**6. Evangelistic church planting.** Though I have already featured the powerful and effective leadership of Bishop Sandy Millar several times, I must mention that Sandy helped pioneer an effective church-planting approach by starting new Anglican congregations in *redundant churches*. In the United Kingdom, churches are redundant in cases where there is a church building but no congregation, or at least not enough of a congregation to support the building, clergy and church life. Rather than selling redundant churches to be used as restaurants or art galleries, Millar and his colleagues began to find, train and deploy young leaders, many harvested out of Alpha, to plant new congregations in these closed churches. I like this kind of thinking and action. This kingdom-based entrepreneurialism and Spirit-inspired faith once again assured me that I can work within the Anglican fold.

### ANCIENT-FUTURE PRACTICES FOR CONTEMPORARY TIMES

Much of the ancient Anglican Church was animated by a missional impulse. In this sense I am doing nothing new as a missionary bishop. I minister in a long line of leaders whose lives and accomplishments overshadow mine. I am simply taking a baton passed along by evangelistically minded Anglican leaders such as Allen, Newbigin, Stott, Packer, Millar, Fullam, Guest, Gumbel and many more.

Anglicanism has the reputation of being rigid and bound by the Book of Common Prayer and the Thirty-Nine Articles. But Anglicanism has also, among its most gifted and courageous leaders, not been afraid to pursue fresh expressions of evangelism and church. The Anglican Church has a way of staying anchored to the ancient tradition while being in tune with the ever-changing times.

Anglicans don't do this merely for the sake of institutional survival, but as a first principle. In fact the preface to the Book of Common Prayer calls for the church, in terms of its mission, to be continually led by the Holy Spirit. Within the framework of keeping the faith whole, the Book of Common Prayer encourages new practices for the sake of "the edification of the people." It allows innovation "according to the various exigency of times and occasions."

The Book of Common Prayer, being the central rule of faith after the Bible, guides and encourages Anglicanism as it adjusts and thrives as a faithful witness to the gospel of the kingdom. The men I have highlighted in this chapter mixed complete orthodoxy with Spirit-led creativity. As I have come to see and know this mix of Spirit and evangelistic entrepreneurialism, I have found a home.

Moreover, I have found a model of leadership. Adjusting and thriving are not accidents. They come from leaders who humbly discern the voice and movement of the Holy Spirit and, having done so, lead with humble confidence. I'd like now to introduce you to two such leaders.

# 13

# Anglican Leadership

*Emmanuel Kolini and John Rucyahana*

Bishop Thad Barnum's book *Never Silent* was one of the means God used to call me to the Anglican Mission. Reading about and then meeting Archbishop Emmanuel Kolini of Rwanda and his good friend and partner Bishop John Rucyahana, along with their wives, Freda and Harriet, saved my eroding confidence in Christian leadership.

Rucyahana is bishop of Shyira diocese in Rwanda. Both he and Archbishop Kolini and their families have been refugees. Having lived through the genocide in Rwanda, they know better than most of us the devastating pain of human evil and the powerful love and deliverance found in the kingdom of God. These men display solidarity with broken humanness that is rarely seen. This instinctual love of others, no matter what it cost them personally, led these bishops to come to the rescue of American Episcopal churches that were religious orphans.

I love and revere Kolini and Rucyahana for many reasons, but I will reflect on just one representative trait that reveals Anglican leadership at its best. The selfless and action-based love of others, which exudes from these two men, is a profound model for young American leaders.

Recently, many church leaders have grown nervous about a dilemma they faced: be an effective leader by means of manipulation, dishonesty and selfishness, or be a godly person without accomplishing much for the sake of the kingdom of God. I know this overstates the case a bit. I'm sure there are those who are simultaneously effective and ethical. Nonetheless, I think I express the concern and apprehension many of us have felt.

For example, think of the leaders interviewed on television. They are usually "models" of some sort. Often they are politicians. They tend to dominate most people's idea of what it means to be a popular, famous and effective leader. Most of the time leaders are willing to say anything, slam anyone and posture any way as a means to their particular end. Both sides of any political, economic and moral debate, appear to be self-aggrandizing, unthinking and morally suspect. I constantly hear these leaders comparing the best of their tribe to the worst of others.

This kind of behavior apparently has invaded all public discourse. It is fundamentally dishonest. It is deceptive and wicked. It is really annoying. And if we stop to think about it, it leads to places most of us do not want to go. It has polluted our whole society and made many young leaders—especially those who aspire to a righteous life—afraid to drink the water of leadership at all. The upcoming generation of Christian leaders don't merely see an unhappy choice, they are deconstructing or fleeing from existing models of leadership.

It has been really sad for me to watch this over the last dozen years. These young women and men, genuine followers of Jesus, have great instincts for connecting to post-Christian culture and wonderful ideas for bringing the kingdom of God to bear on the challenges of their communities. They know how to stay in conversation with their neighborhoods. They have noses for justice. But in many cases they have no desire to publicly implement those ideals for fear of losing their relational and communal values.

I don't think I am quite as affected by this phenomenon as those a bit younger than me. Nonetheless, I found in Archbishop Kolini and Bishop Rucyahana a bright light pointing the way to truly altruistic, successful and valuable leadership that serves the good of others. It is encouraging to see these traits lived out so obviously, passionately and humbly by two key leaders in the global Anglican Church.

Over history the best Anglican leadership, exemplified by Kolini and Rucyahana, has had a certain quality to it that makes it exceptional, including these characteristics: (1) an unassuming nature, (2) a humble sense of one's place in the wider and historical world, (3) the courage to do the right thing, (4) the humility to stay in loving dialogue with others who are difficult or disagreeable, (5) a willingness to hold onto the truth at hand with an epistemological humility that knows there may be more truth (but not transgressing orthodoxy).

Kolini and Rucyahana have literally helped save their nation. They have comforted the afflicted, fed the hungry, freed the guilty, assisted victims and helped set national policy. They are rightly revered, but they never let themselves be consumed by admiration. They are too busy admiring Jesus, participating in his kingdom agenda and working on their own spiritual formation.

I know from my years working with and encouraging nervous young leaders that it is these kinds of values and practices that give them hope, courage and confidence to lead. I see this kind of heart in Archbishop Kolini and Bishop Rucyahana. They boldly get things done. But their personal qualities and the communities they created while executing their work stand like mountain ranges overlooking the oceans of their accomplishments.

Like Archbishop Kolini and Bishop Rucyahana, the Anglican leaders I have respected have a way of going about their work with a remarkable mix of effectiveness and humility. I call this a *sweet reasonableness*.

# 14

# The Spirit of Anglicanism

*A Sweet Reasonableness*

Over the past twenty-five years I have been to England approximately fifteen times. I've been to many parts of the country from the South to the Midlands—but only rarely and briefly to the North. I've also spent a lot of time with British religious leaders on their trips to America. With this bit of groundwork, I am going to tell you a story that will anchor my thoughts in this chapter.

In central London, just down Brompton Road from Holy Trinity Brompton, is a Middle Eastern restaurant I find irresistible. A few years ago, long before I had any inkling I would be an Anglican bishop, I took a young pastor friend there for a late lunch. In the course of the conversation, I found myself saying something I have said scores of times to others: There is a specific and definite *spirit* among the British Anglican evangelicals I have known over the years and have come to appreciate and value. There is a "sweet reasonableness" about most of them. Historically, Anglicanism does not bully but simply sets itself forth. It invites participation, contemplation and conversation. This is a great gift to the postmodern, post-Christendom situation.

This spirit is important to me because I have become weary of the increasingly dogmatic, angry, unkind, un-Christlike, argumentative and dishonest spirit in much of the religious debate in America. Rationalized by a concern for the truth, this harmful spirit flows like a devastating oil spill from certain media outlets, churches and conferences. I can hardly stomach it. I have great empathy and patience with the growing number of people who are leaving churches marked by this spirit.

I know I've just painted with a broad brush. So, in fairness, I should say a couple of things to moderate the last paragraph— as true as it is. First, there are churches for whom those attitudes and practices do not apply. Second, I am not alarmed by "mean-spirited, unreasonable attitudes" because I do not really care about truth. I do believe in and search for truth. I just happen to think that there are no good or appropriate rationalizations for harming others with our words. (I think Jesus, Paul, John and Peter would back me on this.)

My theological heroes within the modern Anglican Church— John Stott, J. I. Packer and Tom Wright—are very concerned for the truth. But they also have outstanding reputations as fair and godly men. My observation, and the point I want to make here about the Anglican spirit, is that this spirit is really timely for both contemporary evangelism and spiritual formation.

Increasingly in our day the medium is the message. It is not enough to demonstrate a concern for the truth and then suppose that such concern baptizes all manner of verbal and attitudinal sin. Spirit and attitude count more than ever. Character is louder than content. What I like so much about the vast majority of Anglican leaders I have met is that their character exemplifies what Jesus had in mind when he said, "Out of the abundance of the heart the mouth speaks" (Matthew 12:34 ESV). What I think is so commendable about Stott, Packer, Wright and others is their heart, and the Spirit-moderated words that flow from it, while their innermost considerations and public comments still hold to the truth as they understand it. The way my British colleagues have spoken to each other over the years has captivated my imagination as a way to conduct myself as a bishop. They provide a stalwart and authoritative alternative to what I have known in other times and places.

## THE SPIRIT OF SERVING OTHERS

If we were playing word association and I said "Anglican" it is likely that the first words said back would be Church of England, archbishop of Canterbury, Book of Common Prayer, episcopal government. This is understandable. But there is much more that lies beneath the surface. Rather than being stuffy and rigid, there is also an engaging sensibleness about the place of the Anglican Church in our changing world. In their book *The Spirit of Anglicanism*, William Wolf, John Booty and Owen Thomas exemplify this openness:

> In order to follow its Lord who became a servant to humanity, the church must be willing to let go its hold upon its self-serving institutionalism. This is not easy. For churches, like all institutions, are notoriously conservative and self-protective. The inability of the church to give

credible evidence of following Christ in this fundamental area is probably the greatest source of people's contempt for and disillusionment with organized religion.

I believe that they are more right in 2010 than when they wrote it in 1979. Today, most young people making first-time decisions to follow Jesus are doing so at least partly within the context of service to others.

This is so because most young people want to partner with the action of God. They want to experience him. But this is not a 1960s-style existential movement. It starts with the assumption that if there is a God, he must be up to something; he must have a plan, a will and an agenda. Theologian David Bosch aptly says:

> The mission of the church as the sent people of God is understood as being derived from the very nature of God. It rightly emerged from the doctrine of the Trinity, not of ecclesiology or soteriology. . . . Mission is not first of all an activity of ours—it is the action of God.

### ANGLICANS LOVE THEIR CHURCH

The enthusiastic Anglicans I have known over the years seemed to me to have an uncommon love for their church. I don't see this same attitude as much in other groups. Some observers even criticize this as a form of elitism. I guess it could be, in its extreme forms. But the evangelical Anglicans I have known love their God and his mission more. This is another area where Anglicans demonstrate a sweet reasonableness, a thoughtful, warm-hearted equilibrium of values.

An observation by the historically celebrated Anglican leader F. D. Maurice is indicative of the way Anglicans hold their love of God, church and the world together in a reasonable manner: "We want to make sure we are not giving people the church, when what they are looking for is the living God. . . . [W]e want people believing in God, not just assenting to doctrine." Evidently, upon reflection, I needed to land in a tribe marked by levelheadedness. It releases me. It makes me feel sane. It gives me hope that we can stay in conversation with an increasingly post-Christian world. Along with orthodox Anglican theology, these attitudes may even frame the bits of glass that make my Anglican bishop mosaic.

As a working pastor, would-be evangelist and missionary bishop, I appreciate that my new Anglican heritage not only provides a sweet reasonableness but also gives me an exciting set of tools to use in the cause of evangelism and discipleship.

# 15

# The Anglican Treasure Chest

Todd, what is the biggest surprise so far in your journey from the Jesus Movement to the Anglican Church?"

I get asked that question a lot. As I've studied Anglicanism for the past couple years and pondered this question, a clear answer has emerged: Anglican theology and practice have given me, as a pastor and church planter, a huge treasure chest of tools for contemporary evangelism and spiritual formation.

As I describe the treasured practices, note that I am not comparing Anglican practices to those of other churches. Instead, I simply feel like a young artist finding grandpa's chest of paint, brushes, watercolors, pastel pencils and sticks of charcoal. And then, of course, not being able to wait to use them, wondering if they are better than the stuff in my bedroom at home. Alternately, I feel like one of the hearers of Ezra as he read the old, forgotten story of God to the Jews after they had made it back to Jerusalem (see Nehemiah 8). They had great joy and a renewed commitment to obedience at the hearing of the Word.

Putting these prized practices to use, we stand in the great tradition of theological growth. God's people experienced God and then reflected on that experience, preserving it in oral and written form so their offspring could benefit from it. I stand in this tradition and hope to pass it on to my children and grandchildren.

I can see this treasure chest of Anglican tools saving contemporary Western faith just as Patrick and his colleagues saved Ireland and Western civilization. I can see the rhythms and routines of Anglican spirituality fitting well the hunger of American seekers.

## LITURGICAL TOOLS UNPACKED

My comments are not a comprehensive analysis but are based on a growing vision of how to effectively engage with the historical practices of the Anglican Church for the sake of others, for the sake of evangelism and for the sake of discipleship to God and his intention for his redeemed people.

At this writing, our new church plant in Costa Mesa, California, has only met for a few months. Slowly, I am introducing Anglican forms of spirituality to a group largely comprising people who had stopped attending church. I am marrying these new practices to the most authentic parts of my rich past: the best of my Bible teaching ideas from Calvary Chapel, the best of worship and a kingdom-based interaction with the person and work of the Holy Spirit from the Vineyard, and the best of the spiritual formation practices I have learned from Richard Foster, Dallas Willard and Eugene Peterson.

Anglican practices have a reputation among most American low-church evangelicals of being fussy and complicated. But as our new church has gotten under way, I have recognized a clear pattern emerging. Many of us are burned out and looking for a fresh way to practice our faith. We are looking for a way of following Jesus that keeps our feet firmly in historic orthodoxy and in conversation with the world.

To us *orthodox* does not mean mere doctrine. It takes into account practices too. These go beyond what we do on Sunday morning to include spiritual practices within our daily routines. We are looking for an orthodoxy that connects us to the world around us. In the context of a congregation pursuing that vision, as I explain historic Anglican practices in uncomplicated, simple terms, the people have grown to love it. We have been given great gifts in our tradition that God is now using in our lives to make us into his cooperative friends in putting the world to rights. The following are some of the tools we are using in Costa Mesa.

**Ancient rhythms.** The liturgical calendar, the lectionary and daily prayers are a source of authority and wisdom. In an era when information is readily available online through thousands of sources, wisdom is highly valued. At a dinner before my ordination to the priesthood I asked Dallas Willard to comment on the ancient Anglican rhythms. He said, "Spontaneity is overrated. Spontaneity only works well when it is rooted in deep practice." He went on to say that every church has a liturgy. The only question is whether it is a good one or not.

**The Book of Common Prayer.** There is an old Latin phrase that is important to our thinking: *Lex orandi, lex credendi*. It is loosely translated "the law of prayer is the law of belief." It calls to mind the connection between prayer/worship and belief. It suggests that right praying leads to right believing, and these lead to right practices, right living. Anglican scholars sometimes put it this way: "The prayer book is conceived not as a book primarily for the clergy [to conduct services], but as the equipment for every layperson in leading the spiritual life."

This tool is not only for the back of pews but also for the followers of Jesus to use daily for shaping their spiritual lives. This is a wonderful vision: the prayer book used by average Christians as a guide to "the happy life, the life well lived, the life which is virtuous, realizing the Kingdom of God on earth."

The Book of Common Prayer is going missional! Leading us by prayer into a kingdom and missional worldview, I see the Book of Common Prayer shaping the community of Jesus one life at time, as we become his cooperative friends, living in creative goodness, through the power of the Holy Spirit, for the sake of others.

***Ministry of the Word.*** The lectionary is a potent tool to shape a worldview, to give seekers a story to embody. In Anglican churches the story of the Bible is told every year through the readings of the lectionary. Without getting uptight or defensive about it, reading and teaching the Bible is right at the heart of historic Anglicanism. Because of the liberal tendencies of much of the Episcopal Church USA, this is not obvious to contemporary observers. But it is nonetheless true of historical Anglicanism, and it is still true in the vast majority of global Anglican churches.

***Creed.*** The creed is a straightforward source of truth amid postmodern epistemological angst. Yet Anglicans are not merely looking for mental assent to doctrines, such as justification by faith. We are looking to love and follow the one who justifies us. We are not looking for the *via media* (middle way) between Rome and Westminster, we are looking for a road that goes beyond positioning to one we can travel in following Jesus. To say the Apostles' or Nicene Creed is to confess alignment with God in the person of Jesus. It is to agree with and participate in the intention of God for humanity. That mental agreement then flows through our hearts and out to our hands and feet for the sake of serving others.

**Prayer of confession and absolution.** The prayer of confession is a compelling source of moral vision. Anyone who daily or weekly prays the following words with sincerity will have a hard time persisting in deliberate sin:

> We confess that we have sinned against you in thought, word and deed, by what we have done and by what we have left undone. . . . We are truly sorry and we humbly repent. . . . [H]ave mercy on us and forgive us; that we may delight in your will and walk in your ways to the glory of your name.

Following confession, the priest offers the prayer of absolution—"God have mercy upon you, pardon and deliver you from all your sins, confirm and strengthen you"—which is a forceful agent of healing, forgiveness and deliverance.

**The peace.** I'll never forget explaining to our growing church the relational and social power of passing the peace in small villages in ancient England, where everyone knew everyone else's business, where everyone had sinned or been sinned against. It is becoming for us a source of relational and communal healing. I've seen families healed as they forgive one another before receiving Eucharist. I've seen terrible ruptures in friendships repaired as people spoke and hugged before receiving bread and wine.

**Eucharist.** Eucharist gives us a growing experience of participation in the life, character formation and mission of Christ. Anglican historian Stephen Neill, connecting Eucharist to the mission of the church, says, "After communion, the church, in union with the Christ whom it has received, offers itself as a living sacrifice to God." Eucharist, with its routines, beauty, rhythms and holiness, does not cause Anglicans to separate *from* the world. It separates us *for* the world. Eucharist leads us into the world, sending us with Spirit power to do acts of mercy and divinely authored works of justice.

*Ordained ministry.* Leadership has fallen on hard times; leaders are increasingly distrusted. After reading or hearing the latest scandal in the news, it is not hard to imagine why this is so. I am seeing in the ordained ministry a chance to model ministry as service to God's agenda in the world and the church. "Once a deacon, always a deacon"—even if one were to become a priest, bishop or archbishop. But deacon-like servant leadership, leadership for the sake of others, has the potential to undo much of the animosity currently directed toward religious leaders.

*Anglican comprehensiveness.* Anglican comprehensiveness is an antidote to the denominational divisiveness that is a complete turn-off to those outside the church. Anglican history has within it three main streams: Anglo-Catholics, with their focus on history and order; evangelicals, with their focus on a present, saving experience of Jesus; and those of the broad church, who say we must avoid the potential divisiveness of partial points of view and learn from each other. That Anglicanism has held these views together for hundreds of years is a little known fact. Were it more widely known, it would be a powerful apologetic for those who cannot stomach the divisiveness in the church.

This is going to be a growth point for me. I have spent my whole ministry in the evangelical, charismatic branch of the church. I know I have things to learn from Anglo-Catholic thought and practice.

Anglican comprehensiveness is not mindless or spineless. It does not mean that all things will be tolerated. It does not lack regard for the truth or for doctrinal precision. Rather, it is grounded in agreement on the fundamentals of the faith. It facilitates dialogue on nonessential issues. It thinks the best of others while maintaining an openness regarding useful practices.

Anglicanism, in committing itself to follow the way of comprehensiveness, has dared to face up to the need to die to what is specifically Anglican in order to be raised up by the power of God in an ecumenically resurrected church comprehensively Christian and human.

In my heart I know that we are *all* united in Jesus and members of his body, the church. I also know that this spirit and attitude is particularly winsome in today's divided world.

### TREASURES FOR THE SAKE OF OTHERS

Archbishop of Canterbury William Temple, who was known for his work toward a just society, famously said, "The church is the only society on earth that exists for the benefit of non-members." And "The task of the church is defined for it. It is the herald and foretaste of the Kingdom of God. For that it exists, and for service to that end it must be organized and equipped." Thus I have taken a vow for my church and for my work as a missionary bishop: I will not take myself and my church's internal political conversations too seriously. I will take God's mission and our vocation in it with all seriousness. To put this into practice I need to visit regularly the Anglican treasure chest of tools for our kingdom and calling as the sent people of God.

# Conclusion

*From Accidental to Purposeful*

Many years ago there was a television commercial for women's hair color by Clairol. According to the famous tagline, "The closer she gets, the better she looks." This has been my experience as I've drawn close to and looked into the Anglican Church.

But my new tribe is not perfect. And I didn't choose Anglicanism because I think every other church is wrong. If I am right, God chose Anglicanism for me. I know we both have blemishes. Even if churches look unblemished from a distance, up close we can see the faint scars, the weary eyes and the strained relationships.

As I've drawn close to the Anglican Church, I've discovered both beauty and blemish. I know it is common today to see the problems and challenges of the Episcopal/Anglican Church in America. We have gone through a lot. I know the experience of frustration, alarm, pain and loss is real. While I only know it secondhand through friends and colleagues, I sincerely empathize with what American Anglicans have been through the last decade or so, and I respect it.

### THE FRUIT OF PURPOSE

While I have had fun with the *accidental* Anglican image, the values, lessons and priorities I have learned through the various stories recounted in this book are not at all accidental. They are carefully chosen and vigorously and cheerfully held. I realize that I am indebted to many Anglican leaders—pastors, professors, evangelists, missiologists, colleagues and friends—who have made my life so rich. How will I honor the debt I owe them? By taking the best of all I have gleaned from them and use it to plant, God willing, hundreds of new Anglican churches on the West Coast.

I am betting the farm on a renewal and revival of religion. We desperately need the enlivening mix of true religious practice married to serving others. To one degree or another, every influential Anglican leader in my life has done this successfully. Picture John Wesley, C. S. Lewis, John Stott, J. I. Packer and N. T. Wright saying morning and evening prayers as bookends to their days—days marked by cheerful service to their families, their students, the people of their congregations and their communities.

Like these examples, innumerable people have found real and lasting life with God through the ancient practices of the church. Word and sacrament have sustained lives of faith and service for as long as there have been Christians.

The birth of the church I lead, Holy Trinity Anglican Church in Costa Mesa, California, has come into being during the

months I have been writing this book. Thus as I come now to
the conclusion I can give some early reports from our bold and
purposeful expedition. The convergence of the evangelical,
Spirit-filled and liturgical elements of Christianity are leading to
the spiritual formation and mission that I dreamed of, worked
toward and hoped for.

I want to let you stand beside me now as I converse with my
friends after church, look over my shoulder to read my emails,
eavesdrop on the comments I have heard walking the hallways.
Forgive me in advance if this seems self-serving. I am showing
you the fruit, not the occasional spot of crabgrass that needs to
be plucked or sprayed with weed-killer.

So here is some representative commentary regarding the *on
purpose* results within the congregation of the accidental bishop.

*"I find Holy Trinity to be a safe place."* Do you find this
to be a bit of an odd statement about a church? I mean how
could a church be *dangerous?* Are we worried that some eight-
year-old boy sprayed WD40 on the slick metal slide, causing
all the kids to zoom down in a big pile, or what? Actually, I
think this comment means guests and members of Holy Trinity are finding safety in the ancient agreement and practice
that is inherent in various elements of liturgy and a commitment to the Bible as God's authoritative and dependable word
for his church. It makes them feel safe that there is not an ecclesiastical Wizard of Oz behind a green curtain reinventing
church every week so that it is more fresh and hip than the
week before. Dechurched people, formerly veteran church attendees, know that such an approach can be simultaneously
exhausting and addicting—and thus dangerous. These same
people find peace and protection in forms of spirituality that

have nourished the church for many hundreds of years.

*"The liturgy is vital."* While I hear this comment quite a bit, it means different things to different people. For some it means *structure*. These people mean to say that they find consistent growth through the rhythms and routines of the liturgy the way athletes find growth in strength, stamina and skill from their workouts. For another group it means *consistency*. This group of people means to point to the reliability and trustworthiness of the words, concepts and worshipful spirit they find in the liturgy. A third representative descriptor I hear is *respect*. This group of people testifies to finding in the liturgy a way to increased reverence for God—a reverence that they tell me is leading to increased love of God and neighbor.

*"I've never knelt before in church."* If you could see the "kneelers" under the hard black chairs we sit in, you would be assured that we not only have an accidental priest, we must also be an accidental church! We bought these high-class gems in bulk from a gardening version of a dollar store. These garden pads are the cheesiest, brightly colored rubber things one could ever lay eyes on—but they are working wonders in our hearts. Several people in our new little church have told me that kneeling is "rewiring my soul" or that "it is developing new levels of humility" or that "I feel myself letting go to God more." I know that one of my favorite parts in Sunday worship is when we all kneel and confess our sins. It is surely true that spiritual worship is bodily—and that such worship goes beyond waving hands and dancing feet to include our knees.

*"I find myself recalling words from the liturgy during the week."* Over the first six months of our church life, as we've grown in our participation in liturgy, we have added bits from

week to week. Not long ago we added an "opening acclamation": "Blessed be God, Father, Son and Holy Spirit . . . and
blessed be his kingdom, now and forever." Why did we do this?
To be more Anglican? To pass a test that certified us as truly liturgical? Nope, for none of those reasons. We added it to say to
ourselves two things every Sunday as we begin to worship. (1)
*Blessed* in this context means to be respected, honored and revered. In the opening acclamation we remind ourselves that
church is not first for us; it is for God. We are not in the room
because we are meeting only with ourselves. We gather to be
with God from the motivation of love, gratitude and reverence.
(2) We are a people created by the kingdom of God—his rule,
reign and grace-filled action on the earth; we are created to
partner with him, serving as his kingdom ambassadors as we
love our neighbors as ourselves. I hear that this simple sentence
is reorienting our lives in meaningful ways.

*"I feel the presence of the Holy Spirit."* In the invocation we
call on God to be manifestly present with us as we engage in
worship, word and Eucharist. Is that because it is the religious
thing to do? Because we want to have Pentecostal street-cred?
No again—none of those motivations. We call on the person
and work of the Holy Spirit because it is what Christians have
done for two thousand years. It is probably the oldest of all
Christian prayers: "Come, Holy Spirit—come give your presence, power and authority, your fruit/character and gifts—give
us hearts to worship you this morning; give us ears to hear your
word; give us hearts to obey what we hear; be generously present to us in Eucharist . . . come, Holy Spirit." There is no such
thing as Christianity without an ongoing, conversational relationship with the Holy Spirit. Weekly, as we begin worship, we

remind ourselves of this. Participants at Holy Trinity who have had no background interacting with the Holy Spirit are finding a powerful new dimension in their lives.

*"Confession is powerful."* Many of us fear God and run from him like Adam in the garden after the original sin. This does no good. When God said in Genesis, "Adam, where are you?" he was not asking for information. Do you picture God like a frantic parent looking for a missing toddler in the clothes racks of a department store? Hardly. It was Adam who was lost and needed to know where he was: separated from God by sin. Week by week as we confess our sin we recognize that we are being found by God, forgiven by him and given freedom, as we pray in the words of the liturgy, to

> send us now into the world in peace,
> and grant us strength and courage
> to love and serve you
> with gladness and singleness of heart;
>     through Christ our Lord.

*"The Creed puts words to my core beliefs."* Every week, after hearing an Old Testament reading, a responsive reading of a psalm, a reading from a New Testament letter and a Gospel reading, and then hearing a sermon based on those readings, we rise to our feet together to publicly confess our faith as we proclaim the Apostles' Creed or the Nicene Creed. Several veteran church attendees have said to me something like: "I have been going to church for much of my life and I have never been clear about what it is we Christians really believe. Saying the creed is giving me intelligent faith for the first time." Others tell me the creed is refreshing their faith and giving them, in the face of growing

secularity, a fresh confidence in the basic truths of Christianity.

These are just some of the highlights of what we are experiencing together. I could not be more pleased and more full of anticipation for the future. We pray that our humble appropriation of liturgy is preparing us to take our place as responsible members of the wider body of Christ.

### WHAT'S YOUR CALLING?

As I have made my way into Anglicanism, I've had a recurring thought: *Anglicans, this is our day!* It's our time to make a significant impact on Western spirituality and ultimately the whole world. It could be that just as God first converted Peter to open the gospel to the Gentile world, he will convert us to bring Christlike religion to our increasingly secularized culture.

Perhaps it's *our turn* to be converted, to step up, take risks and be used by God as his cooperative friends in bringing the world to rights. This is exactly what John Wesley, Richard Hooker, Roland Allen, Lesslie Newbigin and countless others have done. They were converted, spiritually transformed, through the historic practices of the church, and then applied their reformed, grace-given, Spirit-empowered lives to the problems of their day.

What's next? After reading *The Accidental Anglican* I hope you too become cognizant of your own journey with God. Having laughed a little with me, maybe you have gleaned a few tidbits of wisdom. Can you see the mosaic of your own spiritual life coming together? Maybe it leads you to a completely different type of work or maybe even a new denomination. As you connect the dots of your life, you too may find a surprising, seemingly accidental calling of your own.

# Acknowledgments

This is one of my favorite parts of *The Accidental Anglican*. For two years I've wanted to broadcast the names of these influential Anglican people who, in hindsight, created a path for me into the Anglican Church. But someone always needed my talks to be short enough to fit a certain window of time, or an editor would tell me that the names, unknown to most readers, just cluttered up the text. I don't regret tightening up a talk or de-cluttering a paragraph. I've just been sad every time I did—sad that I could not commend to the world those who have positively shaped this accidental bishop.

But at last I get my turn, so here goes . . .

As a young man, influencing me from the background or by their writings, were C. S. Lewis, J. I. Packer, John Stott and Michael Green; I heard John Wimber tell wonderful stories that caused me to admire John Collins and David Watson; later I met David Pytches; then Sandy Millar and then the pastoral leaders of "the Alpha gang" at Holy Trinity Brompton in London: Nicky Gumbel, Nicky Lee and Jamie Haith.

John Mumford and Rick Williams came into my life via an interesting twist: in the eighties a handful of young Church of England leaders felt called into Vineyard churches. John and Rick were two examples. I liked and respected them very much—and still do!

John Guest was an example of an Anglican who preached the gospel in large public settings.

In my tenure as the executive director of Alpha USA I spent a lot of time around pastors of Anglican/Episcopalian churches. The founder of Alpha USA and my predecessor, Ali Hanna, and his wife, Nancy, are extraordinary people of talent, wisdom, grace and generosity. Several Anglican pastors connected to Alpha have become friends and guides into the Anglican world: Kim Swithinbank, Tory Baucum, Tony Baron, Ron McCrary, Steve Wood, John Yates, Keith Andrews and Patrick Wildman. Tony and Patrick now work with me in Churches for the Sake of Others.

Along the path I was also welcomed and helped by colleagues Comforted Keen, Tom Riley and David Bryan.

I want to state my gratitude to the office staff at the Anglican Mission in Pawleys Island, South Carolina, especially Chuck Murphy, his chief of staff Susan Grayson and H. Miller, executive director. Over the last year I have also grown to love my brother bishops: Sandy Greene, Thad Barnum, TJ Johnston, Terrell Glenn, Doc Loomis, Philip Jones; John Miller and Silas Ng.

Having been instrumental in my transition from Alpha to theAM, and having moved from Pawleys Island and working with me now in Churches for the Sake of Others are Ellis and Cynthia Brust. Cynthia is also director of communications for theAM.

Several people in our partners in mission, The Anglican Church in North America, have been especially gracious to me: I think of Bob Duncan along with John Guernsey, Bill Thompson and David Roseberry. I call St. James Anglican Church in Newport Beach, California, my "home away from home." I enjoy my friendship with their clergy Richard Crocker, Cathie Young and Jack Bunting.

No one has had a more transforming effect on my theology than N. T. Wright.

Dennis Bennett and Terry Fullam stand in my mind as especially gifted clergy of the past generation.

I also want to express gratitude to a few Anglican friends who are world-class laypeople and have come alongside me on my journey: David and Tina Segel; John and Rebecca Mackay; Emily Bailey; Ted and Kay Poitras; Mike and Sydney Murphy; Glenn and Suzanne Youngkin.

No one has had a more shaping role in this journey than my new church, Holy Trinity Anglican Church in Costa Mesa, California. They have helped guide the accidental bishop in the ways of Anglican spirituality and mission.

I'm sure I have forgotten a name or two. If you see yourself missing here, just know that my brain and fingers could not get synched up this late at night. Point it out though, and I'll handwrite your name in and give you a signed copy of the book as an apology!

My editor at InterVarsity, Cindy Bunch, has, over the course of three books, become a literary teacher and a true friend—I cannot thank or honor her and her colleagues enough.

Last and most importantly, none of the journey represented by the names affectionately listed above could have happened without the love and partnership of my wife, Debbie. Debbie and our children, Jonathan and Carol, are, humanly speaking, the inspiration for my life and writing.

# A Word from the Author

Weekly, and sometimes daily, I get inquiries about joining with the church-planting work of Churches for the Sake of Others (C4SO). Here in no particular order are the top ten ways to know if you are a good fit:

1. You have not given up on the church.

2. You are motivated to reinvent church around the historic mission of the church and the gospel of the kingdom.

3. You are motivated to be spiritually transformed by the best, most contextually specific use of Word, Spirit, calendar, liturgy and the practices of spiritual formation.

4. You are motivated to launch a congregation of people who become ambassadors of the kingdom, who announce, demonstrate and embody the gospel of the kingdom for the sake of others in acts of social justice, healing and evangelism.

5. You have no present place or feel out of place where you are, and desire to be in a network of like-minded people.

6. You would like to be on the ground floor of such a group and thereby have the corresponding privilege and responsibility of developing its values and practices.

7. You are committed to being a church-planting church, with the goal of planting two new churches every five years for the first ten years. You resonate with the calling to be a part of planting two hundred new churches in the next twenty years.

8. You have read and resonate with the history of the Anglican Mission—especially its Rwandan roots—and the information on the Anglican Mission and C4SO websites.

9. You are creative and are willing to be part of something being invented "on the fly."

10. You share the values and practices associated with evangelistic/missional church planting.

Want to know more? Check us out at www.c4so.org.

# Notes

## Preface

*p. 16*   "Life [is] like a box of chocolates": *Forrest Gump,* dir. Robert Zemeckis (Paramount Pictures, 1994).

## Chapter 1: Life on My Own Terms

*pp. 21-22*   "It is base cowardice to run away from the church": James Lloyd Breck, *James Lloyd Breck: Apostle of the Wilderness,* comp. Charles Breck (Nashota, Wis.: Nashota House, 1992), p. 79. Breck was a noted priest, educator and missionary in the Episcopal Church. Key founder of Nashota House, he is rightly a hero to many—especially to Anglo-Catholics.

*p. 22*   "I have had enough of governing": Ibid., p. 131.

*p. 22*   "I care not for being . . . the head": Ibid., p. 141.

*p. 22*   Atheism is the thought that nothing good is going to happen: I do not know where I heard or read this quote, but it is not original with me.

*p. 23*   "the [ordained] ministry serves the people of God": William J. Wolf, John E. Booty and Owen C. Thomas, *The Spirit of Anglicanism* (Harrisburg, Penn.: Morehouse, 1979), pp. 42-43.

*p. 25*   After experiencing a few personal faith setbacks: I have written about this transition in brief in *Christianity Beyond Belief* (2009) and more extensively in *Giving Church Another Chance* (2010), both by InterVarsity Press.

**Chapter 2: Liturgical Leanings**

*p. 28*        "ancient-future" vibe: See, for instance, Robert E. Webber, *Ancient-Future Faith* (Grand Rapids: Baker Academic, 1999).

**Chapter 4: Shaping a Faith**

*p. 41*        "Packer's ability to address immensely important subjects": Mark A. Noll, "Last Puritan," *Christianity Today,* September 16, 1996 <www.christianitytoday.com/ct/1996/september16/6 ta051.html>.

**Chapter 5: What Is a Rector?**

*p. 47*        "Every authentic ministry begins . . . with the conviction": John Stott, *The Message of 1 & 2 Thessalonians* (Downers Grove, Ill.: InterVarsity Press, 1994), p. 68.

*p. 48*        "the gospel creates": Ibid., p. 20.

*p. 52*        love and connectivity: Here I am working with ideas from Edwin H. Friedman's *A Failure Of Nerve: Leadership in the Age of the Quick Fix* (New York: Seabury, 2007).

**Chapter 6: Following the Holy Spirit in Anglicanism**

*pp. 55-56*    "As you were telling me about the possibility": Rose Madrid-Swetman, email correspondence to author, spring 2008.

**Chapter 7: Ordained a Deacon and Priest**

*p. 60*        "Love like you've never been hurt": Attributed to Satchel Paige. However, many sources attribute the following to Mark Twain: "Sing like no one's listening, love like you've never been hurt, dance like nobody's watching, and live like it's heaven on earth."

*p. 61*        What exactly is ordination: In this context I am not aiming for fully nuanced theological precision but for something more plain and practical.

**Chapter 8: Giving and Receiving the Eucharist**

*p. 69*        "If you wanna know / If he loves you so": Rudy Clark, "Shoop Shoop Song" (1964).

## Chapter 9: Consecrated as a Bishop

*p. 74*  copes and miters: A cope is a long ecclesiastical vestment. A miter is a bishop's headdress.

## Chapter 10: A Story to Embody

*pp. 83-84*  "According to the early Christians, the church doesn't exist": N. T. Wright, *Simply Christian* (San Francisco: HarperSanFrancisco, 2006), p. 204.

*p. 86*  "the aims of Jesus": N. T. Wright, *Jesus and the Victory of God* (Minneapolis: Fortress, 1996). See part 3, "The Aims and Beliefs of Jesus."

*p. 88*  Journey Inward, Journey Outward: This title comes from Elizabeth O'Connor's 1968 book by that title. It is published by Harper & Row.

## Chapter 11: Anglicanism and the Kingdom of God

*p. 91*  "Mission is not so much an activity of the Church": David Jacobus Bosch, *Transforming Mission* (Maryknoll, N.Y.: Orbis, 1998), p. 390.

*p. 91*  "The task of the church is defined for it": William J. Wolf, John E. Booty and Owen C. Thomas, *The Spirit of Anglicanism* (Harrisburg, Penn.: Morehouse, 1979), p. 117.

*p. 92*  "The kingdom of God is never at risk": I have heard Dallas say this many times in private and public settings.

*p. 92*  missional church movement: For example, Darrell L. Guder, ed., *Missional Church: A Vision for the Sending of the Church in North America* (Grand Rapids: Eerdmans, 1998); Alan Hirsch, *The Forgotten Ways: Reactivating the Missional Church* (Grand Rapids: Brazos, 2007); and David E. Fitch, *The Great Giveaway: Reclaiming the Mission of the Church from Big Business, Parachurch Organizations, Psychotherapy, Consumer Capitalism and Other Modern Maladies* (Grand Rapids: Baker Books, 2005).

## Chapter 12: The Anglican Evangelistic Tradition

*p. 96*  Churches for the sake of others: For more on "Churches for the sake of others," see www.c4so.org.

p. 99    Third wave and power evangelism: Peter Wagner coined the term *third wave* to differentiate the Wimber/Vineyard movement from classic turn-of-the-century Pentecostalism and the 1970s charismatic movement. The crucial distinction for Wagner and Wimber was that the Vineyard maintained classic evangelical doctrine concerning baptism in the Holy Spirit, but took on Pentecostal practices. On power evangelism see John Wimber, *Power Evangelism* (Ventura, Calif.: Regal, 2009).

p. 101   Alpha in all fifty U.S. states: In fairness and in the spirit of full disclosure, I served for four years as the executive director of Alpha USA. As of 2010, I continue to serve on the board and executive committee.

p. 102   the Book of Common Prayer encourages new practices: See the opening paragraph of any version of the Book of Common Prayer.

## Chapter 14: The Spirit of Anglicanism

pp. 108-9   "sweet reasonableness": William J. Wolf, John E. Booty and Owen C. Thomas, *The Spirit of Anglicanism* (Harrisburg, Penn.: Morehouse, 1979), p. 177.

pp. 110-11   "In order to follow its Lord who became a servant to humanity": Ibid., p. 182.

p. 111   1960s-style existential movement: The emerging pattern is not philosophically motivated. It does not start with the human self and its actions, assuming self-actualization as the core of human existence. To the contrary, its focus is on God, but not God alone. Its impulse is to experience God most profoundly through serving others. There is of course a down side to this: experience cannot be our only way of knowing.

p. 111   "The mission of the church as the sent people of God": David Bosch, *Missional Renaissance*, pp. 21, 23.

p. 112   "We want to make sure we are not giving people the church": F. D. Maurice, quoted in Wolf, Booty and Thomas, *The Spirit of Anglicanism*, p. 81.

## Chapter 15: The Anglican Treasure Chest

*p. 114*  Patrick and his colleagues saved Ireland and Western civilization: See Thomas Cahill's *How the Irish Saved Civilization* (New York: Doubleday, 1995).

*p. 115*  "Spontaneity is overrated": Malcolm Gladwell's *Outliers* has recently demonstrated a similar idea: it takes ten thousand hours of practice to be expert at any task.

*pp. 115-16*  "The prayer book is conceived not": William J. Wolf, John E. Booty and Owen C. Thomas, *The Spirit of Anglicanism* (Harrisburg, Penn.: Morehouse, 1979), p. 161.

*p. 116*  "the happy life, the life well lived": Ibid., p. 35.

*p. 116*  cooperative friends . . . for the sake of others: For a full description of these four phrases see my *Christianity Beyond Belief* (Downers Grove, Ill.: InterVarsity Press, 2009).

*p. 116*  liberal tendencies of much of the Episcopal Church: I have no specific quarrel with anything or anyone in the Episcopal Church USA. This is a simple and widely acknowledged observation.

*pp. 117-18*  "After communion, the church, in union with the Christ": Stephen Neill, *Anglicanism* (New York: Oxford University Press, 1977), p. 77.

*p. 118*  we must avoid the potential divisiveness of partial points of view: I am aware that the recent "church plants" that have come out of the Episcopal Church USA (i.e., ACNA, CANA, theAM) but remain within the worldwide Anglican Communion is to some observers a departure from this history. Space and editorial focus do not permit analysis here. But both the blogosphere and Amazon.com are rich sources of comments and book-length treatments on the subject.

*p. 119*  "Anglicanism, in committing itself to follow the way of comprehensiveness": Wolf, Booty and Thomas, *Spirit of Anglicanism*, p. 117.

*p. 119*  "The church is the only society on earth": William Temple, quoted in ibid.

**Conclusion**

*p. 121*        Innumerable people have found real and lasting life with God:
                To be fair, many others have found the ancient practices of the
                church dry as dust. But the reasons for this do not set aside my
                basic point. See my *Giving Church Another Chance* (Downers
                Grove, Ill.: InterVarsity Press, 2010) for an extended discussion
                on this point.